Port Moody Public Library

学做中国菜
Learn to Cook Chinese Dishes
家宴类　　Family Banquet

外 文 出 版 社
FOREIGN LANGUAGES PRESS

前　言

朱熙钧

　　倘不是想成为专业厨师，只是为了自家享用或偶尔飨客而学做中国菜，是无须拜师学艺的。中国主妇们的厨艺最初几乎都是从她们的老祖母那里耳濡目染学来的；待到为人妻母之后，她们之中的一些有心人或借助菜谱潜心揣摩，或与友邻切磋交流，制作出的菜馔有时竟然不逊于出自名店名厨之手的。当然，在中国的家庭中，擅长烹饪的男士也不在少数，而且饭店中的名厨以男性居多。

　　这套《学做中国菜》丛书的编撰者都是在名店主厨的烹饪大师。为了使初学者易于入门，他们以简明的文字介绍了每一菜式的用料、刀法、制作步骤等。读者只须按所列一一去做，无须多日便可熟能生巧，举一反三，厨艺大进。

　　《学做中国菜》系列丛书共九册，包括水产类、肉菜类、菜蔬类、豆品类、汤菜类、冷菜类、米面类、禽蛋类和家宴类。本册为《学做中国菜》系列丛书之一，介绍4套家庭宴席菜肴。

　　约几位亲朋来家中小聚，聊聊天，听听音乐，再备几样菜肴，吃顿便餐，真是其乐融融。

　　自备家宴虽不及在餐馆设宴中规中矩，但是，在家中主客可以无拘无束，菜肴的品种，菜量的多少，口味的调配等可以随心所欲。纵使主人的烹调技艺略逊于专业厨师，客人一般不但不会苛求，反而会同主人共享自己动手的乐趣；更何况常常还会歪打正着，烹制出意想不到的风味的菜馔，胜过名店的料理。

　　本册菜谱列有家宴单四式，每式选配菜品十种。宴客时可视就餐人数选择其中一式，也可从各式菜单中各选几种重新组合。选配菜品时须注意荤菜与素菜、主食与副食、冷盘与热菜等的合理搭配，还应考虑到来客的年龄、籍贯、嗜好等因素。如果客人中有老人和孩子，就需备有几样松软酥烂、清淡爽口的菜肴，而且其余菜中尽量少放辛辣调料；一般生长在中国南方的人喜食鱼、虾，口味偏于清淡，而北方人爱吃牛、羊肉和浓酽味重的菜，在备宴时应兼顾来客们的不同喜好。不过随着社会交往的日趋频繁，地域间的饮食差异正在缩小，一席家宴若能兼有南北中西菜肴，往往会平添几许新奇和乐趣。其次，所选菜品还应合乎宴客的时令，如时值夏季应以清爽素淡的菜品为主，不宜过于油腻，秋冬则应多选配富含热量的菜肴，并可添加一两样有刺激性的辛辣食品。最后，对于应邀赴宴客人特殊的饮食习惯和禁忌应预先有所了解，以避免在餐桌上出现尴尬场面。

Foreword

Zhu Xijun

You don't have to take lessons from a professional teacher to learn the art of Chinese cooking if all you want to do is to entertain your friends or cook for your family. Almost without exception, Chinese women learn this skill by watching and working together with their mothers or grandmothers. After they become wives or mothers themselves, the most diligent among them will try to improve their techniques by consulting cook books and exchanging experiences with their neighbors. In this way they eventually become as skilled as the best chefs in established restaurants. It should be noted, of course, that most of the well-known chefs in famous restaurants are men because many men in Chinese homes are just as good at the art of cooking as their wives.

This book in the *Learn to Cook Chinese Dishes* series have been compiled by master chefs. They have used simple explanations to introduce the ingredients, the ways of cutting, and the cooking procedures for each Chinese recipe. Readers who follow the directions will before long become skilled in the art of Chinese cooking. The entire set consists of nine volumes, covering freshwater and seafood dishes, meat dishes, vegetable dishes, courses made from soy beans, soups, cold dishes, pastries, dishes of eggs and poultry, and recipes for family feasts. This particular volume presents four sets of family feast dishes.

Though a family feast is not as standard as a formal dinner in a restaurant, hosts and guests can enjoy a meal at home prepared according to their own tastes and one consisting of quantities and varieties according to their own liking. Even if the host cook is somewhat less skilled than a restaurant cook, the guests are unlikely to complain and may even add pleasure by joining the host in preparing the meal. Very often, some unexpectedly fine dishes are created in a home kitchen.

Each set of the family feasts introduced in this book consists of ten dishes. You can choose any one of them according to the number of diners or you can select from each of the four sets to create your own combination. You should, however, pay attention to the balance between meat dishes and vegetable dishes, staple food and non-staple food, cold dishes and warm dishes. Besides, you are advised to take into consideration the age, native place and dietary habits of your guests. If your guest diners include old people and children, the feast should include some soft and less greasy dishes. Furthermore, dishes should be less spicy. In China for example, southerners like fish and shrimp with light seasonings while northerners love beef, mutton and heavily seasoned food. This regional difference in diet, however, is lessening as a result of the increased movement of the people and social contacts. A feast consisting of both northern and southern dishes will always add pleasure and achieve better results. Still, the choice of dishes should coincide with the season. In summer, lightly seasoned dishes as opposed to oily dishes should be the main courses; while in autumn, dishes should contain more calories and a dinner should have one or two spicy dishes. Finally, the host should have information on the dietary habits, particularly dietary taboos of the guests in order to avoid any awkwardness at the dinner table.

目　录
Contents

名词解释
Terms Used in Chinese Cooking ·············· (1)

8—10 人宴席(A)
Family Feast for 8 to 10 People (Type A) ········ (8 - 26)

冷盘一组
Cold Dishes ···················· (8)

翡翠虾仁
Shrimps with Green Peppers ·············· (10)

植物四宝
Four Vegetable Delights ·············· (12)

香酥牛肉卷
Crispy Beef Roll ················· (14)

蟹粉豆腐
Bean Curd with Crab Meat ·············· (16)

糖醋鱼
Sweet and Sour Fish ················ (18)

葵花鳗鱼
River Eel in Sunflower Shape ············ (20)

烤鸡
Roast Chicken ·················· (22)

黄桥烧饼
Sesame Cake Huangqiao Style ············ (24)

火腿竹荪汤
Ham and Bamboo Fungus Soup ·············· (26)

8—10 人宴席(B)
Family Feast for 8 to 10 People (Type B) ········ (28 - 46)

九子冷盘
Nine Cold Dishes ················· (28)

宫保鸡丁
Stir-fried Chicken with Chili Sauce and Peanuts ··· (30)

芝麻虾球
Shrimp Balls with Sesame ·············· (32)

回锅肉片
Twice-cooked Pork with Spicy Sauce ·········· (34)

葱爆鸭丝
Quick-fried Shredded Duck with Scallions ·········· (36)

松鼠鱼
Sweet and Sour Fish in Squirrel Shape ··········· (38)

什锦素菜包
Assorted Vegetables Wrapped in Lettuce ·········· (40)

淀粉虾饺
Steamed Dumpling with Shrimp ·············· (42)

花篮烧麦
Flowery Steamed Dumpling ············· (44)

六生火锅
Six-meat Hotpot ·········· (46)

5—7 人宴席(A)
Family Feast for 5 to 7 People (Type A) ········· (48 – 66)

六味冷碟
Six Cold Dishes ·········· (48)

白灼基围虾
Boiled Shrimp ·········· (50)

松仁玉米
Pine Nuts with Sweet Corn ·········· (52)

荷叶粉蒸肉
Pork and Rice Wrapped with Lotus Leaves ········· (54)

西瓜鸡
Tender Chicken in Watermelon ·········· (56)

炒素什锦
Mixed Vegetables ·········· (58)

火腿桂鱼
Mandarin Fish with Ham ·········· (60)

花色蒸饺
Steamed Dumpling in Flower Shape ·········· (62)

开花馒头
Flowery Steamed Bun ·········· (64)

鸳鸯莼菜汤
Mandarin Duck and Water Shield Soup ·········· (66)

5—7 人宴席(B)
Family Feast for 5 to 7 People (Type B) ········· (68 – 86)

荤素五拼盘
Assorted Five Appetizers ·········· (68)

宫灯虾仁
Shrimp in Lantern Shape ·········· (70)

火腿湘莲
Ham with Lotus Seed ·········· (72)

龙井鱼片
Dragon Well Fish Slices ·········· (74)

太极双丝
Pork with Vegetables ·········· (76)

蛋皮烧麦
Steamed Dumpling Wrapped with Egg ·········· (78)

蘑菇菜心
Green Vegetables with Mushrooms ·········· (80)

三鲜蒸饺
Steamed Dumpling with Pork and Shrimp ·········· (82)

寿桃包子
Steamed Longevity Peach ·········· (84)

三丝清汤
Combination Meat Shreds Soup ·········· (86)

计量换算表
A comparison of the weight systems and a conversion table for measuring Chinese cooking ingredients ······ (88)

名词解释 Terms Used in Chinese Cooking

上浆：猪肉丝、猪肉片、牛肉丝、牛肉片、羊肉丝、羊肉片、鸡肉片在烹制前都要上浆。上浆大多用于滑溜、滑炒、清炒、酱爆等烹调方法。上浆好坏，直接影响烹调出菜肴的质量。上浆就是把切好的肉，用水冲洗净，放入盐、料酒、淀粉(有时也放鸡蛋)，拌匀后，向一个方向搅拌，感到有劲为止。

Coating (*shangjiang*): Shreds and slices of pork, beef, mutton and chicken have to be coated before they are cooked in such ways as slippery-frying, quick-frying and stir-frying. And how the meat is coated has a direct bearing on the quality of the cooked dish. The coating process involves first washing the cut meat, then adding in salt, cooking wine, and cornstarch(sometimes eggs are also used) and stiring well in the same direction until you feel it is a bit sticky.

刀工 **Cutting techniques:**

直刀法：就是指刀同砧板垂直的刀法，分切、剁、砍、切是一般用于无骨的主料，剁是将无骨的主料制成茸的一种刀法，砍通常用于加工带骨的或硬的主料。

Straight-cutting: Holding the knife perpendicularly over the chopping board to cut, chop and heavy-cut the main ingredient. Cutting is applied to boneless meat ingredients, chopping is done to turn boneless ingredients into pulp or paste and heavy-cutting is used when preparing meat with bones or other hard ingredients.

平刀法：是刀面与砧板平行的一种刀法，分推刀、拉刀。推刀就是把刀从刀尖一直推到刀根，拉刀就是把刀从刀根拉到刀尖。平切就是把刀一切到底。

Horizontal-cutting: Holding the knife flat against the chopping board to push it or pull it through the ingredients.Pushing means to push the knife through the ingredients from the knife's tip through to its end while pulling involves going through the ingredients from the end to the tip of the knife.

斜刀法：刀面同砧板面成小于90度夹角的刀法。

Slashing: To cut by holding the knife in an angle smaller than 90 degrees from the surface of the chopping board.

花刀：是在主料表面用横、竖两种刀法的不同变化，切(不断)出花纹，经加热后，主料卷曲成各种形状的刀法，有菊花形花刀，麦穗刀，鳞毛形花刀等。

Mixed cutting: To cut straight and then cross with sideways cuts to produce varied patterns. When heated, the ingredients cut in this way will roll up into different forms such as chrysanthemums, wheat ears and scales, according to the ways they are cut.

片：用切或片的方法将原料加工成薄片。质地硬的原料用切，质地软的用片的方法加工成薄片。

Slicing (*pian*):By either cutting or slicing to turn the ingredients into thin slices. Hard ingredients require cutting while soft ingredients require slicing.

丝：丝有粗细之分，一般在0.2-0.4厘米左右。一般先将主料切成0.2-0.4厘米的薄片，再将这些薄片排成瓦楞状，排叠要整齐，左手按稳主料，不可滑动，用刀把主料切成丝。

Shredding (*si*): The thickness of shreds usually varies between 0.2 (0±08 in) and 0.4 cm (0±16 in). First, either chunks of meat or vegetables are cut into thin slices of 0.2 to 0.4 cm in thickness. The slices are then arranged neatly like roof tiles.Pressed steadily underneath the left hand of the chef, the slices are finally cut into shreds.

条：条的成形方法，是先把主料切成厚片，再将片切成条，条的粗细取决于片的厚薄。

Strapping (*tiao*):Main raw materials are cut into thick slices that are cut again into straps the size of which is decided by the thickness of the slices.

粒：粒比丁小些一般在0.3厘米见方，切的方法同丁相同。

Grain-sized dicing (*li*): Cut in the same way as diced pieces, they are simply much smaller in size. The most common size is 0.3 cm (0.12 in) each side.

丁：先将主料切成厚片，再将厚片切成条，然后再切成丁。丁有大小之分，大丁在2厘米见方，小丁在1厘米见方。

Dicing (*ding*): Main raw materials are cut into thick slices that are cut into straps. In turn, the straps are reduced to diced pieces that may be as large as 2 cm (0.8in) on each side or as small as 1 cm (0.39 in) on each side.

末：末比粒还小，将丁或粒剁碎就可以了。

Mincing (*mo*): Ground ingredients are even smaller than grain-sized dices.Usually the diced pieces are chopped into mince.

茸：用排剁的方法把主料剁得比末还细。

Chopping to make a pulp (*rong*): To chop the materials, knife cut after knife cut into pieces even finer than minced materials.

块：块是采用切、砍、剁等刀法加工而成的。块分菱形块、方块、长方块、滚刀块等。

Cutting into chunks (*kuai*): Chunks are the result of perpendicular and sideways cutting as well as chopping. The chunks come in many shapes such as diamonds, squares and rectangles.

炸：是旺火加热，以食油为传热介质烹调方法，特点是火旺用油量多。

Deep-frying (*zha*): Heat the cooking oil over a hot fire and deep-fry the materials. This process is characterized by a hot fire and a large amount of oil.

炒：炒是将加工成丁、丝、条、球等小型主料投入油锅中，在旺火上急速翻炒成熟的一种烹调方法。炒分滑炒、熟炒、干炒等几种。滑炒是经过粗加工的小型主料先经上浆，再用少量油在旺火上急速翻炒，最后以湿淀粉勾芡的方法，叫滑炒。熟炒是把经过初步加工后的半成品，改切成片或块，不上浆，用旺火烧锅热油，放入半成品翻炒，再加佐料而成。煸炒和干炒是把主料煸一下，在热油锅急火炒至退水后，加佐料，起锅。

Stir-frying (*chao*): Put processed materials in the shape of diced pieces, shreds, straps, or balls into the heated oil and quickly stir them over a hot fire. There are several different ways of stir-frying. *Hua chao* (stir-frying with batter), for example, requires that the ingredients are put in a batter and then quickly stirred in a small quantity of oil over a hot fire.The final process is to apply the mixture of cornstarch and water. *Shu chao* (stir-frying precooked food) does not require that the materials be put into some kind of batter. Simply put the precooked materials into the wok and use a hot fire before adding spicing agents. *Bian chao* and *gan chao* (raw stir-frying) calls for the simmering of main ingredients, then quick-stir-frying over a hot fire until the juice is fully absorbed. Now add spicing agents and the dish is ready to serve.

溜：溜是先将主料用炸的方法加热成熟，然后把调制好的卤汁浇淋于主料上，或将主料投入卤汁中搅拌的一种烹调方法。
Slippery-frying(*liu*): First deep-fry the main ingredient and then top it with sauce or mix the main ingredient in the sauce.

爆：爆是将脆性主料投入适量的油锅中，用旺火高油温快速加热的一种烹调方法。
Quick-fry over high heat (*bao*): Put crispy materials into the wok with medium amount of oil and quickly stir the materials over high heat.

隔水炖：隔水加热使主料成熟的方法，叫做隔水炖。
Steaming in a container (*ge shui dun*): Put the main ingredient into a bowl or similar container and cook it in a steamer.

烧：烧是经过炸、煎、煸炒或水煮的主料，再用葱姜炝锅后，倒入翻炒，然后加适量汤水和调味品，用旺火烧开、中小火烧透入味，改用旺火使卤汁稠浓的一种烹调方法。
Stewing over medium,then high heat (*shao*): After putting scallions and ginger into the wok, put in the main materials that have been deep-fried, or stir-fried or boiled and stirred. Then add water and seasoning materials to cook over a hot fire until the ingredients boil. Turn the fire to medium or low to allow full absorption of the sauce into the ingredients before turning the fire hot again to thicken the sauce.

扒：扒是将经过初步熟处理的主料整齐地排放在锅内，加汤汁和调味品，用旺火烧开、小火烧透入味，出锅前，原汁勾芡的一种烹调方法。
Stewing and adding thickening (*pa*): Neatly arrange the main ingredient that has already been cooked,add water and flavoring materials and cook over a hot fire until it boils. Turn the fire to low to allow full absorption of the flavor. Thicken the sauce with the mixture of water and cornstarch before bringing the dish out of the wok to serve.

煮：煮是将主料放入多量的汤汁或水中、先用旺火煮沸、再用中小火烧熟的一种烹调方法。
Boiling (*zhu*): Put main materials of the dish into the wok with an adequate amount of water and cook it over a hot fire to the boiling point. Then continue to cook after turning the fire to low or medium.

烩：将加工成片、丝、条、丁等料的多种主料放在一起，烩锅翻炒后，用旺火制成半汤半菜的菜肴，这种烹调方法就是烩。
Precooking and then stewing (*hui*): First heat the oil in the wok, put in scallions and ginger and then put several kinds of main ingredients that have been cut into slices, shreds, chunks or dices to cook over a hot fire so as to create a dish of half soup and half vegetables and meat.

煎：煎是以少量油布遍锅底、用小火将主料煎熟使两面呈黄色的烹调方法。

Sauteing (*jian*): Put a small amount of oil into the wok and use a low fire to cook the main ingredient until it is golden brown on both sides.

蒸：蒸是以蒸汽的热力使经过调味的主料成熟或酥烂入味的烹调方法。

Steaming (*zheng*): Cook the materials that have already been prepared with flavoring agents by using hot steam.

拔丝：拔丝又叫拉丝，是将经过油炸的小型主料，挂上能拔出丝来的糖浆的一种烹调方法。

Crisp frying with syrup (*ba si*): Put small-size ingredients that have already been deep-fried into sugar syrup heated in the wok. When diners pick up the materials, long sugar threads are created.

焯水：就是把经过初加工的主料，放在水锅中加热至沸(主要为去腥味或异味)，原料出水后供烹调菜肴之用。焯水分冷水锅和热水锅。冷水锅就是主料与冷水同时下锅，水沸取出，适用于腥气重血量多的主料如牛肉、羊肉等。热水锅就是先将锅中水加热至沸，再将主料下锅，翻滚后再取出主料。适用于腥气小，血污少的主料如鸡、鸭、猪肉和蔬菜。

Quick boiling (*chao*): Put main ingredients into the pot and heat the water to boiling point(in order to remove fishy or other undesirable smells). Then cook the boiled ingredients. The quick-boiling process includes cold water boiling and hot water boiling. The former requires putting the ingredients into the pot toge ther with the cold water and then taking them out when the water boils. This process is often applied to such materials as beef and mutton,which contain a fishy smell and a lot of blood. The latter calls for heating the water in the pot to boiling point before putting the ingredients in.This is applicable to materials like chicken, duck, pork and vegetables that have a much weaker fishy smell and less blood.

油温表

油温类型	俗　　称	油温特点
温油锅	四成 70℃-100℃	无青烟，无响声，油面平静。
热油锅	五、六成热 110℃-170℃	微有青烟，油四周向内翻动。
旺油锅	七、八成热 180℃-220℃	有青烟，油面仍较平静，用勺搅动有响声。

Temperatures of cooking oil:

Category	Temperature	Features
Luke-warm	70ºC-100ºC 158ºF-212ºF	Smokeless, soundless, calm oil surface
Hot oil	110ºC-170ºC 230ºF-338ºF	Slight smoke, oil stirs from the side to the center of the wok
Very hot oil	180ºC-220ºC 356ºF-428ºF	Smokes, the surface remains calm and when stirred, sizzling sound is heard.

花椒：花椒是花椒树的果实，以籽小，壳厚紫色为好。味香麻，烹调肉类的调料。

Prickly ash (*hua jiao*): Seeds from prickly ash trees, which are small and light purple in color. They have a slight effect of numbness on the tongue. Used to cook dishes with meat.

椒盐：味香麻，是炸菜蘸食的调味品。把花椒和盐按1:3的比例在锅中，微火炒成焦黄，磨成细末，即成。

Pepper salt (*jiao yan*): This mixture is made by stirring one portion of peppercorns and three portions of salt in the wok until they turn crispy yellowish in color and release their fragrance. Then finely grind the mixture into powder. It serves as a seasoning for deep-fried dishes.

味精： 根据个人口味，也可不放味精，而使用适量的鸡精。
Monosodium glutamate and chicken bouillon: Though MSG is essential in traditional Chinese cooking, for many who do not find it agreeable, chicken bouillon can be used instead.

茴香： 小茴香是茴香菜的籽，呈灰色，似稻粒，有浓郁的香味。
Fennel seeds (*hui xiang*): Seeds of fennel plants, grey in color and similar to unhusked rice grains in shape, have a hot flavor.

大茴香： 又名八角、大料，形如星状，味甜浓，烹调肉类的调料。
Star anise (*da hui xiang*): In the shape of stars, they have a strong and sweet flavor. Mostly used in cooking meat dishes.

糟： 制作料酒剩下的酒糟经过加工就成为烹调用的糟，糟具有同料酒同样的调味作用。
Steaming with distillers'grains sauce (*zao*): Distillers'grains, which are left over from liquor making, are processed into a spicy agent for cooking that has the same function as the cooking wine.

五香料： 大料、茴香、桂皮、甘草、丁香(丁香花蕾)五种香料

混合为五香料，研成粉为五香粉。
Five Spices (*wu xiang liao*): A mixture of powdered star anise, fennel seed, cinnamon bark, licorice root and clove buds. Also referred to as the "five-powdered spices".

桂皮： 是桂树的皮，外皮粗糙呈现褐色。
Cinnamon (*gui pi*): The bark of cinnamon trees, brown in color.

料酒： 常用料酒是用糯米等粮食酿制成的，料酒，在烹调菜肴过程中起去腥、增香的作用，特别是烹制水产或肉类时少不了它。如没有料酒，可用适量的啤酒或白兰地代替，但没有料酒好。
Cooking wine (*liao jiu*): Cooking wine, brewed from grain, is applied to remove the fishy smell and increase the aroma of the dish. It is particularly essential when cooking dishes with aquatic ingredients and meat. While cooking wine is most desirable, in its absence, beer and brandy can be used.

勾芡： 勾芡就是在菜肴接近成熟时，将调好的湿淀粉加入锅内，搅拌均匀，使卤汁稠浓。增加卤汁对主料的附着力的一种方法。
Thickening with mixture of cornstarch and water (*gou qian*): When the dish is nearly cooked, put a previously prepared mixture

of cornstarch and water into the dish and stir well so as to thicken the sauce or broth. This process promotes the flavored sauce to stay with the main materials of the dish.

勾芡作用：1、增加菜肴汤汁的粘性和浓度。2、增加菜肴的光泽。

Major functions of this process: (1) Increase the stickiness and thickness of the sauce of the dish. (2) Making the dish look more shiny.

勾芡关键：1、勾芡必须在菜肴即将成熟时候进行。2、勾芡时锅中汤汁不可太多或太少。3、必须在菜肴的口味、颜色已经调准后进行。4、勾芡时锅中油不宜太多。

Key for using this process: (1) This process must be conducted when the cooking of the dish is nearly complete. (2) The sauce in the wok must not be too much or too little when this thickening technique is applied. (3) This process can only be done after all efforts for flavoring and coloring of the dish are completed. (4) When doing the thickening process, the wok should not have too much oil in it.

如何使用筷子

吃中式饭菜一般使用筷子。筷子是用木或竹、骨及其它材料制成长 25~30 厘米、上方（各边为 8 毫米）下圆（直径为 3~5 毫米）的二根小棍。

使用时须依靠拇指及食指、中指和无名指的连贯配合。方法是：首先把两根筷子拿在右手，用食指、中指及无名指在距筷子近上端处各夹一根筷子，再把拇指和食指合在一起，如图 1。用筷子取食时，把食指和中指夹的一根向上抬，另一根不动，使两根筷子张开。如图 2。夹取食物时，把食指和中指夹的筷子往下压，夹住食物，抬起筷子进食，如图 3。

How to Use Chopsticks

Chopsticks for eating Chinese food are usually made from wood, bamboo, animal bones or other materials. About 25 to 30

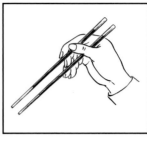

(1)

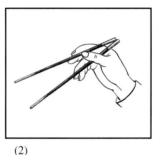

(2)

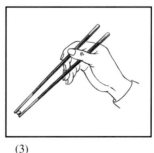

(3)

centimeters long, their top is square, about 0.8 square centimeter, and the low end round with a diameter of 3 to 5 millimeters.

The correct way of using the chopsticks requires concerted efforts of the thumb, index finger, middle finger and third finger. Hold the pair of chopsticks in the right hand, using the index finger, middle and third fingers to keep the chopsticks steady near their top and then push them open by moving the thumb and index finger. (See Drawing 1)

To pick things up with chopsticks, lift upward one of the two chopsticks with the index and middle fingers while keeping the other one where it is so as to separate the two. (See Drawing 2)

Once the chopsticks have picked up the food, press one of the chopsticks with the thumb and index finger and raise the pair. (See Drawing 3)

笼屉 蒸锅
Steaming tray(*long ti*)Usually made of bamboo or wood, these often come in several tiers

炒锅
Skillet

火锅
Hot-pot

砂锅
Earthen pot

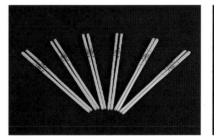

汤勺 炒铲 漏勺
Soup spoon Shovel Perforated spoon

筷子
Chopsticks

菜（面）板
Chopping board

8－10人宴席（A）

第一道菜：冷盘一组
第二道菜：翡翠虾仁
第三道菜：植物四宝
第四道菜：香酥牛肉卷
第五道菜：蟹粉豆腐
第六道菜：糖醋鱼
第七道菜：葵花鳗鱼
第八道菜：烤鸡
点　　心：黄桥烧饼
　　汤：　火腿竹荪汤

冷盘一组

金鸡报晓拼盘（由凉拌胡萝卜、黄瓜、鸡蛋清、松花蛋、熏鱼、春笋、烤鸡等熟菜拼成）
围蝶由鸡、毛豆、海蛰、果汁浸冬瓜、苦瓜、牛肉组成。

Family Feast for 8 to 10 People

(Type A)
Course 1: Cold Dishes
Course 2: Shrimps with Green Peppers
Course 3: Four Vegetable Delights
Course 4: Crispy Beef Roll
Course 5: Bean Curd with Crab Meat
Course 6: Sweet and Sour Fish
Course 7: River Eel in Sunflower Shape
Course 8: Roast Chicken
Pastry: Sesame Cake Huangqiao Style
Soup: Ham and Bamboo Fungus Soup

Cold Dishes

The Golden Rooster Assorted Cold Foods (made with pre-cooked carrots, cucumbers, egg white, preserved duck eggs, smoked fish, spring bamboo shoots and roast chicken)

Surrounding Cold Dishes: Chicken, Boiled Tender Soy Beans, Shredded Jelly Fish, Wax Gourd with Lemon Juice, Balsam Pear and Sliced Beef

翡翠虾仁

主料：虾仁 300 克。

辅料：青椒 10 只、熟火腿末 5 克。

调料：清汤 50 克、料酒 15 克、盐 6 克、糖 3 克、味精 2 克、湿淀粉 15 克、淀粉 20 克、油 250 克（实耗 100 克）、鸡蛋清 1 只。

制作：①虾仁洗净，滤干水份放盐 4 克、鸡蛋清、淀粉上浆备用。

②青椒选灯笼形，去蒂籽，洗净用刀在蒂口周围刻成花瓣型，滤干水。

③将炒锅置中火烧热，倒入油烧至四成热时，倒入青椒炸至呈翠绿色，倒出油后，锅中加水 150 克，味精 1 克、盐 2 克，翻烧 1 分钟，倒出青椒滤干水份，口朝上，排在盘中备用。

④锅置火上，放油 25 克，油热至五成，倒入虾仁翻炒，放清汤、料酒、味精 1 克调好口味，放入湿淀粉勾芡，翻炒、淋麻油起锅，装入青椒中，撒上火腿末即成。

特点：绿白相间，造型美观。

口味：鲜美滑嫩

Shrimps with Green Peppers

Ingredients:

300 grams (0.66lb) shrimps
10 green peppers
5 grams (0.18oz) cooked ham, minced
50 grams (3tbsp) water
15 grams (3tsp) cooking wine
6 grams (1tsp) salt
3 grams (2/3tsp) sugar
2 grams (1/2tsp) MSG
15 grams (1tbsp) mixture of cornstarch and water
20 grams (4tbsp) dry cornstarch
250 grams (1 cup) oil (only 100 g or 7tbsp to be consumed)
1 egg white

Directions:

1. Wash the shrimps clean, drain them and mix with 4 g (2/3 tsp) of salt, the egg white and dry cornstarch.

2. Select the lantern-shaped green peppers, remove their stems and seeds, wash them clean, and cut petal-shaped patterns around where the stems used to be.

3. Heat the cooking oil until it is about 70-100℃ (160-210℉). Put in the green peppers and cook until they turn bright green. Pour out the oil, add 150 g (10tbsp) of water, 1 g (1/4tsp) of MSG and 2 g (1/3tsp) of salt to stir-fry for one minute. Take out the green peppers and place them on a plate, keeping their opening in view.

4. Put 25 g (1 2/3tbsp) of oil in the wok and heat until it is about 110-135℃ (230-275℉). Put in the shrimps and stir-fry. Add the water, cooking wine, and 1 g (1/4tsp) of MSG and pour in the cornstarch-water mixture to thicken the sauce. Keep stir-frying. Sprinkle a few drops of sesame oil and put the green peppers into the wok. Spread the minced ham on the shrimps and green peppers and the dish is ready to serve.

Features: The white and green colors as well as the shapes of the green peppers and shrimps form nice combinations.
Taste: Refreshing and succulent.

翡翠虾仁
Shrimps with Green Peppers

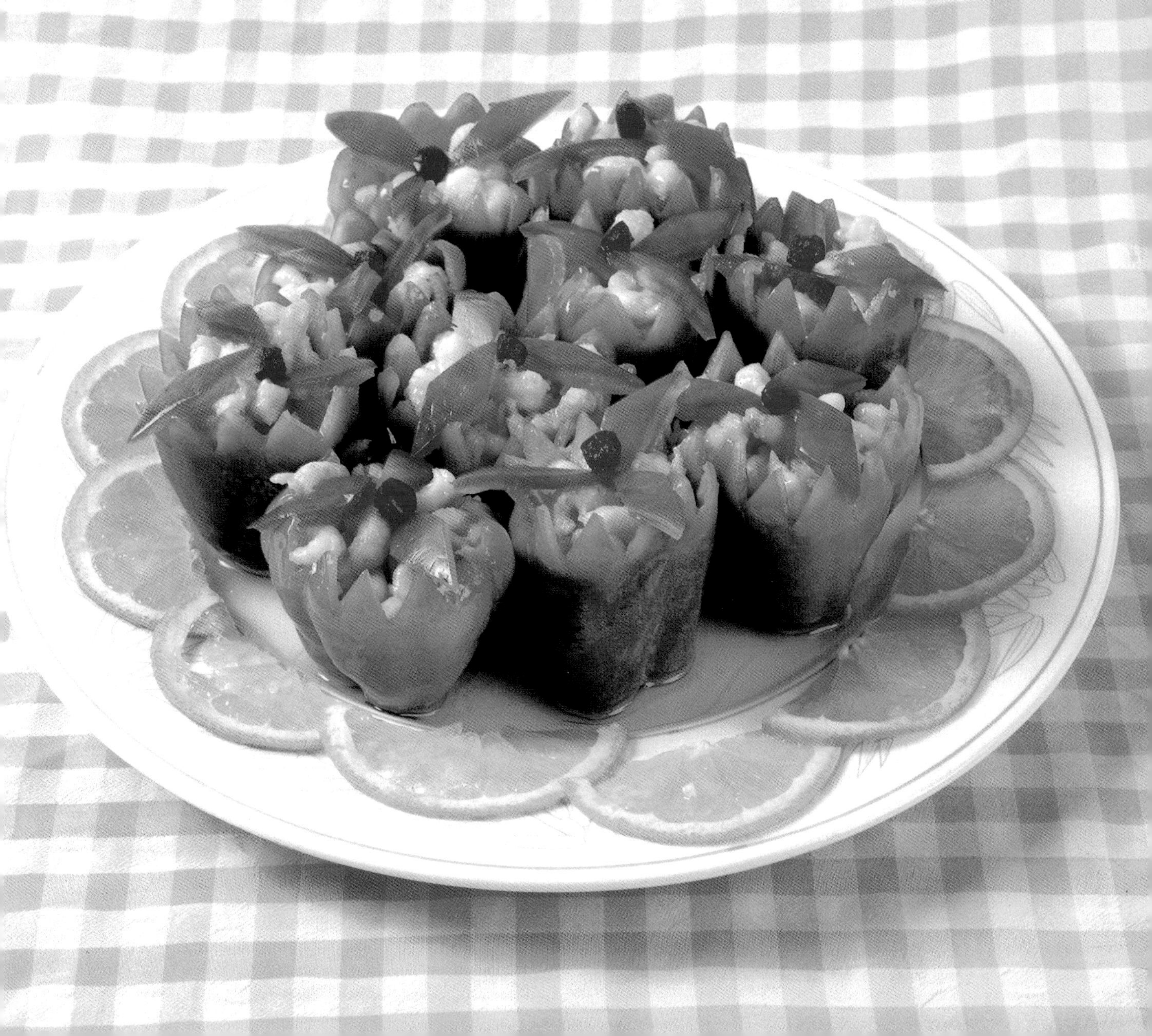

植物四宝

主料：新鲜蘑菇（或罐装）150 克、罐装玉米笋 150、胡萝卜 150 克、丝瓜 150 克

辅料：青菜心 10 棵

调料：盐 5 克、味精 2 克、鸡汤 200 克、油 200 克、湿淀粉 60 克

制作：①在蘑菇伞面刻"十"字花刀，玉米笋一分为二，胡萝卜去皮后切成圆片，丝瓜去皮，剖开后去瓤切成凌形块，菜心洗净去根备用。

②锅烧热加油 40 克，烧至五成热时倒入蘑菇翻炒后加盐 1 克，味精 0.4 克，鸡汤 50 克，烧透后倒入 15 克湿淀粉勾芡，淋油出锅装盘

③用上述方法分别将玉米笋、胡萝卜、丝瓜、青菜心烧熟。将四品种分类放在盘中用菜心将它们分开即成。

特点：色泽鲜艳、五彩分明

口味：咸鲜

Four Vegetable Delights

Ingredients：

150 grams (0.33 lb) fresh or canned mushrooms
150 grams (0.33 lb) canned baby corn
150 grams (0.33 lb) carrots
150 grams (0.33 lb) towel gourd
10 pieces tender green vegetables
5 grams (5/6 tsp) salt
2 grams (1/2 tsp) MSG
200 grams (2/5 cup) chicken soup
200 grams (14 tbsp) oil
60 grams (3 tbsp) mixture of cornstarch and water

Directions：

1. Make a cross cut on top of each mushroom, cut each baby corn in half, cut the carrots into round slices, remove the skin and pulp of the towel gourd and then cut it into diamond-shaped chunks. Remove the roots of the tender green vegetables.

2. Heat 40 g (3 tbsp) of oil to 110-135℃ (230-275℉) and put in the mushrooms to stir-fry. Add 1 g (1/6 tsp) of salt, 4/5 g (1/10 tsp) of MSG and 50 g (3 tbsp) of chicken soup and boil well. Use 15 g (1 3/4 tbsp) of the cornstarch-water mixture to thicken the soup. Sprinkle on a few drops of oil and then take out the mushrooms and place them on a plate.

3. Use the same method to separately cook the baby corn, carrots, towel gourd and vegetables. Put the mushrooms, corn, carrots, and towel gourd separately around the edge of a serving plate, and place green vegetables between them to keep them apart.

Features：Beautifully colored.
Taste：Salty and refreshing.

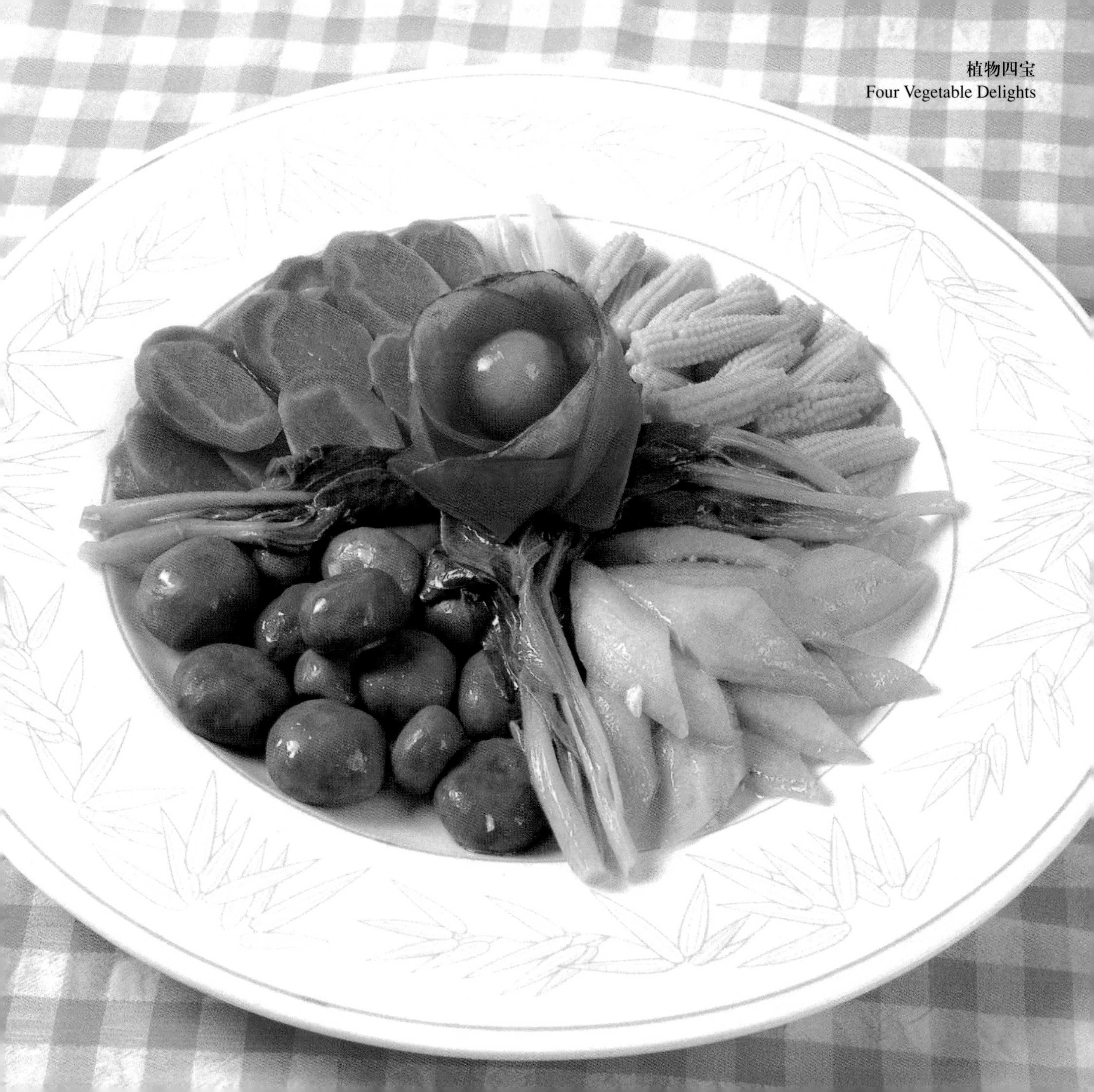
植物四宝
Four Vegetable Delights

香酥牛肉卷

主料：牛肉末 300 克

辅料：面包屑 350 克

调料：鸡蛋 2 只、味精 1 克、盐 2 克、料酒 10 克、葱、姜末各 5 克、干淀粉 10 克、油 300 克

制作：①牛肉末加盐、味清、料酒、葱姜末、干淀粉 5 克搅拌上浆待用。

②鸡蛋磕入碗内打成蛋液。

③将浆好的牛肉末分成 3 份搓成直径 5 厘米、长 15 厘米的条状放入盘中上笼旺火蒸熟取出,冷却后均匀地裹上蛋液再粘上面包屑待用。

④炒锅烧热加入油,烧至五成热时,投入牛肉卷炸至外表呈金黄色倒出沥油。

⑤将牛肉卷切成 3 厘米长的斜刀块装盘。

特点：色泽金黄

口味：外酥里嫩,香味浓郁

Crispy Beef Roll

Ingredients：
300 grams (0.66 lb) ground beef
350 grams (0.77 lb) bread crumbs
2 eggs
1 gram (1/4 tsp) MSG
2 grams (1/3 tsp) salt
10 grams (2 tsp) cooking wine
5 grams (1/6 oz) finely cut scallions
5 grams (1/6 oz) chopped ginger
10 grams (1 1/2 tbsp) dry cornstarch
300 grams (1 1/5 cup) cooking oil

Directions：

1. Add to the ground beef the salt, MSG, cooking wine, scallions, ginger and 5 g (1 tbsp) of the dry cornstarch, and mix well until it becmes sticky.

2. Whip the eggs in a bowl.

3. Divide the ground beef into 3 portions and shape into long rolls 5 cm (2 inches) in diameter and 15 cm (6 inches) in length. Steam over strong fire for 10 minutes. When the rolls cool off, cover them with the whipped egg and bread crumbs.

4. Heat the oil in a wok to 110-135℃ (230-275˚F) and deep-fry the beef rolls until they are a golden color. Drain off the oil.

5. Cut in a slanting way to divide the rolls into sections 3 cm (1.2 inches) long each. Put on a plate and serve.

Features：Golden in color.
Taste：Crispy outside and tender inside, the rolls are really delicious.

蟹粉豆腐

主料：豆腐 400 克，蟹 1 只约 250 克

调料：葱姜末各 5 克、盐 2 克、味精 1 克、胡椒粉 0.5 克、麻油 2 克、色拉油 50 克、香醋 5 克、料酒 5 克、鸡汤 150 克、湿淀粉 5 克

制作：①将蟹洗净上笼蒸熟，剥出蟹肉蟹黄弃除壳待用。②豆腐切成 1.5 厘米见方的丁，用沸水煮一下捞出，用清水漂清。

③炒锅烧热，下油加热至八成下葱姜爆出香味，倒入蟹肉，略炒，烹入料酒，放入香醋，倒入鸡汤煮沸后放入豆腐丁，下盐、味精改小火烧 5 分钟，用湿淀粉勾芡，出锅装盘淋上麻油，撒上胡椒粉即可。

特点：色泽金黄

口味：鲜嫩爽滑，香味浓郁

Bean Curd with Crab Meat

Ingredients:

400 grams (0.88 lb) bean curd
1 crab weighing about 250 grams (0.55 lb)
5 grams (1/6 oz) finely cut scallions
5 grams (1/6 oz) chopped ginger
2 grams (1/3 tsp) salt
1 gram (1/4 tsp) MSG
1/2 gram (1/10 tsp) pepper powder
2 grams (2/5 tsp) sesame oil
5 grams (1 tsp) vinegar
5 grams (1 tsp) cooking wine
50 grams (3 1/2 tbsp) salad oil
150 grams (3/5 cup) chicken soup
5 grams (1 tsp) mixture of cornstarch and water

Directions:

1. Wash and steam the crab until it is done. Take out the crab meat (both the white and reddish parts). Get rid of the shell.

2. Cut the bean curd into dices 1.5 cm ((0.6 inch) long on each side. Quick-boil in water and then run through cold water to wash clean.

3. Heat the oil in a wok to 200-220℃ (390-430°F) and stir-fry the scallions and ginger until they produce a distinctive aroma. Add the crab meat and quickly stir several times. Add the cooking wine, vinegar and chicken soup and bring to a boil. Add the bean curd, salt and MSG, and cook for 5 minutes over a low fire. Thicken the sauce with the mixture of cornstarch and water. Sprinkle on the sesame oil and take out to serve.

Features: Nice looking with shiny yellowish color.
Taste: Refreshing, tasty and succulent.

蟹粉豆腐
Bean Curd with Crab Meat

糖醋鱼

主料：黄鱼 1 条（约 750 克）。

调料：番茄酱 150 克、油 500 克（实耗 100 克）、白醋 50 克、糖 150 克、盐 6 克、蒜茸 2 克、味精 2 克、清汤 100 克、淀粉 150 克、湿淀粉 50 克、料酒 25 克。

制作：①鱼杀洗干净、用刀在鱼身上正反两面各平行划 4 刀，然后用盐 4 克和料酒腌渍 15 分钟。
②在腌渍后的鱼的两面拍上淀粉，抖去余粉备用。

③旺火热锅，放油，待油温升至七成热时，把鱼投入油锅炸至金黄色后，倒出滤油，装入盘中。
④锅内留余油 10 克，加热后，放入蒜茸炒出香味，再放番茄酱、盐 2 克、味精、清汤、白醋调好口味，倒入湿淀粉勾芡，出锅浇在炸好的鱼身上即可。

特点：色泽金红色，造型美观
口味：外脆里嫩，鱼肉鲜香，卤汁甜酸可口

Sweet and Sour Fish

Ingredients：
1 seawater fish (yellow croacker) (about 750 grams or 1.65 lb)
150 grams (8 tbsp) tomato sauce
500 grams (2 cups) oil (only 100 g or 7 tbsp to be consumed)
50 grams (3 tbsp) white vinegar
150 (11.5 tbsp) grams sugar
6 grams (1 tsp) salt
2 grams (1/15 oz) minced garlic
2 grams (1/2 tsp) MSG
100 grams (6 tbsp) water
150 grams (3/4 cup) dry cornstarch
50 grams (2 2/3 tbsp) mixture of cornstarch and water
25 grams (1 3/4 tbsp) cooking wine

Directions：
1. Clean the fish and on each side make four horizontal cuts. Marinate the fish with 4 g (2/3tsp) of salt and the cooking wine.

2. Dust the fish with dry cornstarch on both sides and then shake off the unnecessary cornstarch that does not stick to the fish.

3. Heat the oil until about 180-200℃ (355-390℉). Put in the fish to deep-fry and then take it out when it is golden brown in color.

4. Leave 10 g (2tsp) of oil in the wok and fry the minced garlic until it releases its aromatic smell. Add the tomato sauce, sugar, 2 g (1/3tsp) of salt, MSG, water and vinegar. Put in the cornstarch-water mixture to thicken the sauce. Now place the fish on a plate to serve.

Features：Golden in color and beautiful in shape.
Taste：Crispy outside and tender inside. The fish is refreshingly tasty and the sauce is invitingly sweet and sour.

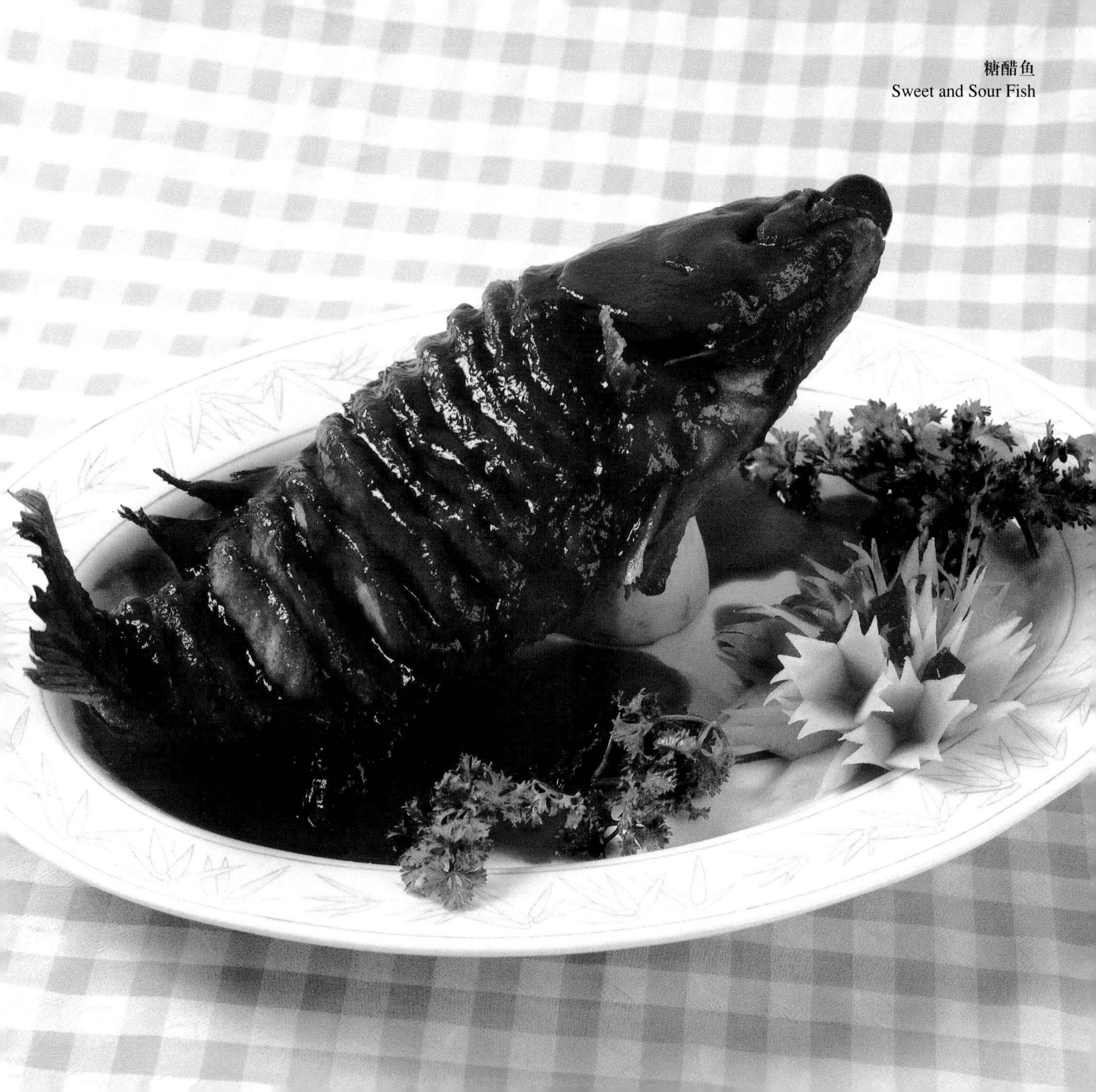

糖醋鱼
Sweet and Sour Fish

葵花鳗鱼

主料：河鳗 1 条（约 500 克）

辅料：干红辣椒 1 只

调料：葱花姜末各 5 克、料酒 20 克、盐 3 克、味精 1 克、蒜茸 10 克、油 10 克

制作：①河鳗去肉脏洗杀干净，切成 0.5 厘米厚的片，然后放盐、味精、料酒腌半小时。辣椒去籽、蒂，洗净，切成 0.8 厘米长的段。

②取一圆盘，将鳗鱼片一片重叠一片由外至内围成一个个同心圆直至排满盘子，撒上葱花、姜末、辣椒、油 5 克，上笼屉用旺火蒸 15 分钟。

③锅置旺火上放油，待油温升至四成热时投入蒜茸翻炒出香味后，淋在鳗鱼上即可。

特点：形似葵花

口味：肉质肥嫩鲜美

River Eel in Sunflower Shape

Ingredients：

1 river eel (about 500 grams)

1 dry red chili

5 grams (1/6 oz) finely cut scallions

5 grams (1/6 oz) chopped ginger

20 grams (4 tsp) cooking wine

3 grams (1/2 tsp) salt

1 gram (1/4 tsp) MSG

10 grams (1/3 oz) mashed garlic

10 grams (2 tsp) cooking oil

Directions：

1. Remove the insides of the eel and cut it into slices half cm (0.2 inch) thick. Marinate with salt, MSG and cooking wine for half an hour. Remove the stem and seeds from the chili, wash clean and cut into sections 0.8 cm (0.32 inch) long.

2. Carefully place the eel slices on a plate to form a circle, each with one end touching the others like the spokes of a wheel or petals of a sunflower. Sprinkle on the scallions, ginger, chili, 5 g (1 tsp) of cooking oil and steam over strong fire for 15 minutes.

3. Heat the remaining oil in a wok to 70-100℃ (160-210℉) and stir-fry the mashed garlic till it produces a strong aroma. Sprinkle the garlic on the eel slices and the dish is done.

Features：The dish is in a beautiful sunflower shape.

Taste：Tender and delicious.

烤鸡

主料：净膛嫩母鸡一只（约 1250 克）

辅料：香菇 20 克、笋 20 克、水发莲子 20 克、酱瓜 20 克、鲜百合 15 克、鲜虾仁 20 克、干贝 15 克、熟火腿 30 克、猪网油 2 张（猪腹内网状隔膜）

调料：油 25 克、甜面酱 15 克、葱、姜汁各 20 克、糖 2.5 克、盐 2 克、味精 1.5 克、料酒 20 克、清汤 10 克、饴糖水 2000 克

制作：①炒锅置旺火烧热，倒入油，待油温升至 4 成热时放入甜面酱、葱姜汁、糖、盐、味精、料酒、清汤，烧开后熄火，制成甜酱汁待用。干贝用温水发好。将香菇、笋、莲子、百合洗净。

②将鸡洗净控干水，将甜酱汁倒入鸡腹内放入盆中腌渍 30 分钟，倒出。

③将香菇、笋、酱瓜、百合、虾仁、干贝、火腿均切成丁。

④炒锅置旺火上，倒入甜酱汁，加入莲子及各种丁翻炒收汁后制成馅，填入鸡腹内，用针线将鸡腹口缝合后浸入饴糖水中上色。

⑤将鸡取出用猪网油包起来，上烤箱烧烤 30 分钟。烤时要不停地翻动，至鸡皮呈酱红色即可。

特点：嫩香鲜肥
口味：咸鲜适口，回味带甜

Roast Chicken

Ingredients：
1 tender hen (about 1250 g or 2.75 lb), inside removed
20 grams (2/3 oz) mushrooms
20 grams (2/3 oz) bamboo shoots
20 grams (2/3 oz) lotus seeds previously soaked in water
20 grams (2/3 oz) pickled cucumbers
15 grams (1/2 oz) fresh lilies
20 grams (2/3 oz) shelled fresh shrimps
15 grams (1/2 oz) scallops
30 grams (1 oz) cooked ham
25 grams (1 2/3 tbsp) cooking oil
15 grams (1 3/4 tsp) sweet soy bean paste
20 grams (2/3 oz) scallion juice (from soaking chopped scallions)
20 grams (2/3 oz) ginger juice (from soaking chopped ginger)
2 1/2 grams (2/5-3/5 tsp) sugar
2 grams (1/3 tsp) salt
1 1/2 grams (1/3 tsp) MSG
20 grams (1 2/3 tbsp) cooking wine
10 grams (2 tsp) water
2,000 grams (8 cups) mixture of water with maltose sugar

Directions：

1. Heat the oil in a wok over strong fire to 70-100℃ (160-210˚F) and add the sweet soy bean paste, scallion juice and ginger juice, sugar, salt, MSG, cooking wine and water, and bring to a boil. Turn off the fire and keep the sauce for later use.

2. Wash the chicken clean and drain off the water. Put the sauce into the chicken belly. Place the chicken in a basin to marinate for 30 minutes. Pour out the sauce.

3. Cut the mushrooms, bamboo shoots, cucumbers, lilies, shrimps, scallops and ham into small dices.

4. Heat the wok, pour in the sauce, add the lotus seed and the mixture of dices, and keep turning until the sauce is absorbed. Use the mixture as stuffing to put into the chicken belly. Sow up the belly and soak the chicken in the mixture of water with maltose sugar for coloring.

5. Take out the chicken, rub oil on it and put in an oven to roast for 30 minutes. It has to be kept turning in the oven until the skin turns brown.

Features：Tender and juice.
Taste：Salty and delicious with a slight sweet touch.

烤鸡
Roast Chicken

黄桥烧饼

主料：面粉 250 克、猪板油丁（生猪油）150 克、熟猪油 50 克

辅料：葱 50 克、火腿丁 20 克、芝麻 100 克、酵母粉（鲜酵母也可，一般超市有售）5 克

制法：①取 150 克面粉加酵母拌匀，再加温水和成面团，醒置 30 分钟，将剩余面粉加熟猪油和成油酥面团。
②葱切末，加入火腿丁、板油丁拌匀，制成馅心。
③将发好的面团揉透、揿扁，放入油酥，沿周边打摺捏紧收口后再揿扁擀成长方形的薄片，重新叠为三层，再擀成长方形后，紧紧卷成圆条形，再摘成每只 50 克的坯子，压扁，擀成圆面皮；面皮上放入馅心捏紧收口，用手掌压成圆饼形，饼面上涂一层清水，粘上芝麻备用。
④烘箱加热至 250 度，放入烧饼生坯，烘制十分钟即可。

特点：香酥可口
口味：咸鲜

Sesame Cake Huangqiao Style

Ingredients：
250 grams (0.55 lb) wheat flour
150 grams (0.33 lb) uncooked pork fat
50 grams (0.11 lb) cooked pork fat
50 grams (1 2/3 oz) scallions
20 grams (2/3 oz) diced ham
100 grams (0.22 lb) sesame seeds
5 grams (1 tsp) yeast powder

Directions：
1. Mix the yeast with 150 g (0.33 lb) of the wheat flour, and add lukewarm water to make into dough. Put aside for 30 minutes. Mix the remaining flour with the cooked pork fat.

2. Finely cut the scallions, mix well with diced ham and uncooked pork fat to use as filling.

3. Roll the dough well. Flatten it and put it on top of the mixture of flour and pork fat. Seal from the surroundings and fold the whole piece of dough into a rectangular shape, flatten it by pressing it. Fold it over three times and press into a rectangular shape once again. Now roll into a thin and long shape. Cut into pieces 50 g (0.11 lb) each. Press these to make wrappings. Put the filling in the middle of each wrapping and seal the edges. Use your hand to press each into a small flat round cake. Sprinkle some cold water onto the raw cake and apply sesame seeds on the wet side.

4. Heat the oven to 250 degrees and bake the cakes for 10 minutes.

Features：Crispy.
Taste：Salty and delicious.

黄桥烧饼
Sesame Cake Huangqiao Style

火腿竹荪汤

主料：水发竹荪 150 克（注：竹荪是著名天然食用菌菇之一，主要产于我国西南地区，生于砍伐过的竹林中，罐装竹荪国内外超市有售）

辅料：火腿 50 克

调料：盐 2 克、味精 1 克、油 5 克、胡椒粉 0.5 克、鸡汤 500 克

制作：①将火腿放入开水中浸泡十分钟，然后洗干净切去黄色的肥膘，上笼蒸熟后取出冷却，再切成薄片。

②竹荪洗净切成 3 厘米长的段备用。

③锅上火加鸡汤、盐、味精、火腿、竹荪烧开后，撒上胡椒粉，淋油即成。

特点：汤清味浓

口味：竹荪脆嫩、清香

Ham and Bamboo Fungus Soup

Ingredients：
150 grams (0.33 lb) soaked bamboo fungus (This edible natural fungus is found in groves with felled bamboo plants and is often available in cans in grocery stores outside China)
50 grams (0.11 lb) ham
2 grams (1/3 tsp) salt
1 gram (1/4 tsp) MSG
5 grams (1 tsp) cooking oil
1/2 gram (1/10 tsp) pepper powder
500 grams (2 cup) chicken soup

Directions：
1. Soak the ham for 10 minutes in hot water, wash clean, remove the yellowish fat part and steam. When it cools off, cut it into thin slices.

2. Wash the bamboo fungus clean and cut it into sections 3 cm (1.2 inches) long.

3. Add the chicken soup to the pot, put in the salt, MSG, ham and bamboo fungus. When liquid starts to boil, sprinkle on the pepper powder and cooking oil. It is now ready to serve.

Features：The soup looks clear, but is richly flavored.
Taste：The bamboo fungus is tender and refreshing.

火腿竹荪汤

Ham and Bamboo Fungus Soup

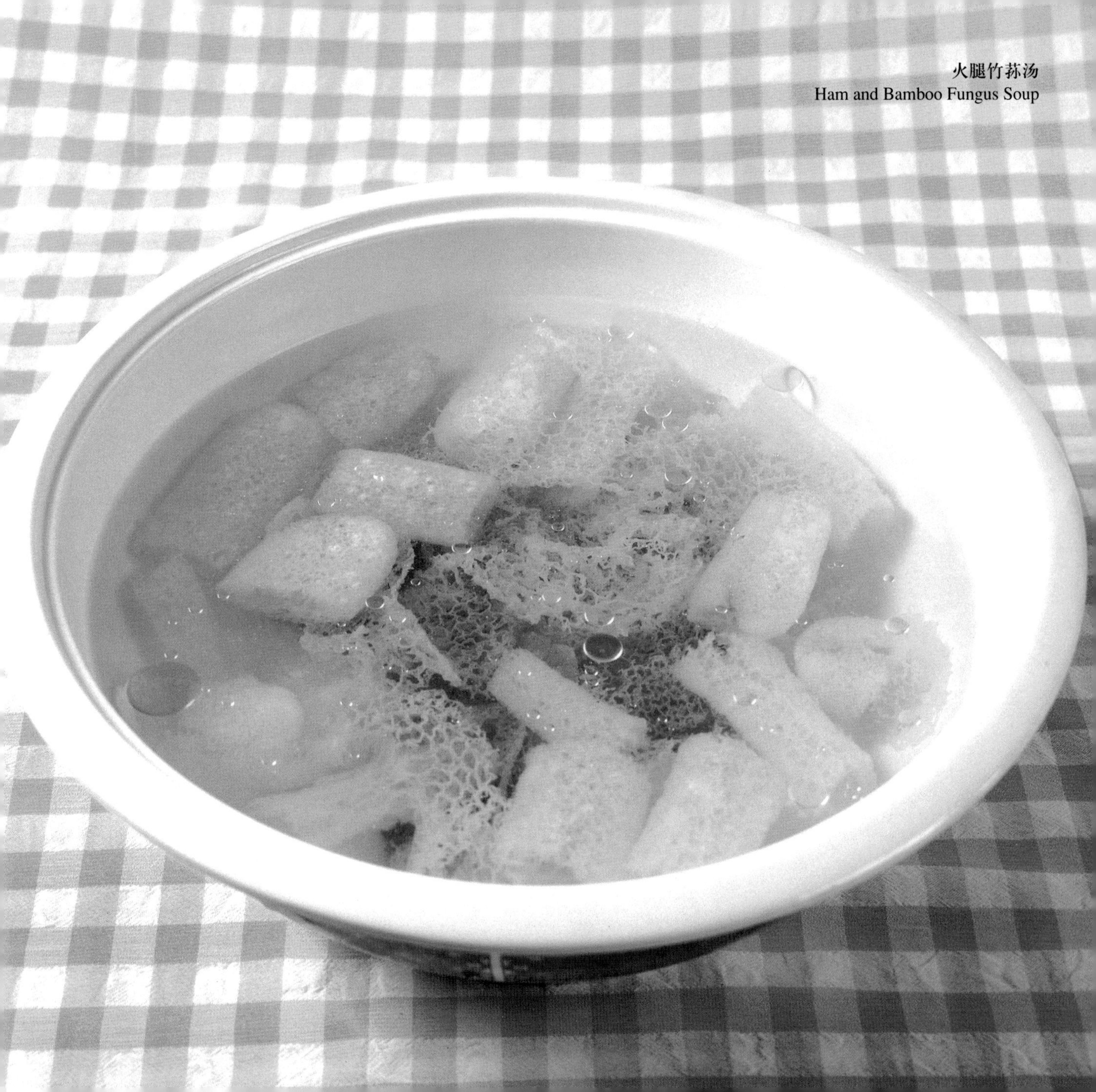

8－10 人宴席（B）

第一道菜：九子冷盘
第二道菜：宫保鸡丁
第三道菜：芝麻虾球
第四道菜：回锅肉片
第五道菜：葱爆鸭丝
第六道菜：松鼠鱼
第七道菜：什锦素菜包
第八道菜：淀粉虾饺
点　　心：花篮烧麦
汤　　锅：六生火锅

九子冷盘

油爆大虾、凉拌葱油海蛰、海米拌丝瓜、五香熏鱼、香干拌芹菜、酱牛肉、蒜茸拌黄瓜、白斩鸡、金丝瓜

Family Feast for 8 to 10 People

(Type B)

Course 1：Nine Cold Dishes
Course 2：Stir-fried Chicken with Chili Sauce and Peanuts
Course 3：Shrimp Balls with Sesame
Course 4：Twice-cooked Pork with Spicy Sauce
Course 5：Quick-fried Shredded Duck with Scallions
Course 6：Sweet and Sour Fish in Squirrel Shape
Course 7：Assorted Vegetables Wrapped in Lettuce
Course 8：Steamed Dumpling with Shrimp
Pastry：Flowery Steamed Dumpling
Soup：Six-meat Hotpot

Nine Cold Dishes

Stir-fried Prawns, Shredded Jelly Fish with Scallion Oil, Dried Shrimp with Towel Gourd, Five-flavor Smoked Fish, Celery with Bean Curd Cheese, Beef Slices, Cucumber with Mashed Garlic, Soy Tender Chicken and Wax Gourd with Lemon Juice

宫保鸡丁

主料：鸡脯肉 250 克

辅料：花生米 150 克

调料：油 500 克（实耗 75 克）、鸡蛋清 1 只、干淀粉 12 克、盐 2 克、味精 1 克、酱油 10 克、糖 10 克、干红辣椒 2 只、葱、姜末各 2 克、清汤 50 克、料酒 5 克、麻油 5 克

制作：①将鸡脯肉拍松，刻上十字花刀，切成 1.5 厘米见方的丁，放入碗内，加入鸡蛋清、盐 2 克、干淀粉 10 克搅拌上浆。余下淀粉用水化开备用。花生米去皮后入油锅炒熟。干红辣椒切成长 1 厘米长的段。

②炒锅置旺火上烧热，放入油，烧至四成热时，放入浆好的鸡丁滑炒至断生，倒入漏勺中，控净油。

③锅内留油 25 克烧热，放入葱姜末、干红辣椒段煸炒出香味，放入清汤、料酒、酱油、糖、味精烧开后，用湿淀粉勾芡，倒入炒好的鸡丁及花生米，翻炒均匀，淋上麻油，装盘即成。

特点：色泽红亮

口味：香辣可口

Stir-fried Chicken with Chili Sauce and Peanuts

Ingredients：

250 grams (0.55 lb) chicken breast
150 grams (0.33 lb) peanuts
500 grams (1 cup) oil (only 75 g or 5 tbsp to be consumed)
1 egg white
12 g (1 2/3 tbsp) dry cornstarch
2 grams (1/3 tsp) salt
1 gram (1/4 tsp) MSG
10 grams (1 1/2 tsp) soy sauce
10 grams (2 tsp) sugar
2 dried red chilies
2 grams (1/15 oz) finely cut scallions
2 grams (1/15 oz) chopped ginger
50 grams (3 tbsp) water
5 grams (1 tsp) cooking wine
5 grams (1 tsp) sesame oil

Directions：

1. Beat the chicken breast with the side of a kitchen knife to soften the texture of the meat. Cut lightly to make cross-cuts on the meat. Then cut the chicken breast into cubes 1.5 cm (0.6 inch) wide each side. Place in a bowl. Add the egg white, 2 g (1/3 tsp) of salt and 10 g (1 tbsp) of dry cornstarch and mix well. Mix the rest of the dry cornstarch with water for later use. Fry the peanuts. Cut the red chilies into fine chips.

2. Heat the oil in a wok to 70-100℃ (160-210°F) and slippery-fry the chicken cubes for 1-2 minutes. Take out and drain off the oil in a strainer.

3. Put 25 g (1 2/3 tbsp) of oil in the wok and stir-fry the scallions, ginger and red chili until they produce a strong aroma. Put in the water, cooking wine, soy sauce, sugar and MSG, and bring to boil. Thicken the sauce with the mixture of cornstarch and water. Put in the chicken and peanuts and turn several times. Sprinkle on sesame oil and dish is ready to serve.

Features：Shiny with brown color.
Taste：Spicy, fragrant and delicious.

宫保鸡丁
Stir-fried Chicken with Chili Sauce and Peanuts

芝麻虾球

主料：虾仁 450 克

辅料：白芝麻 50 克、鸡蛋清 2 只

调料：料酒 5 克、味精 1 克、淀粉 10 克、油 350 克（实耗 150 克）、盐 3 克

制作：①将虾仁洗净，滤干水份，放盐 3 克、鸡蛋清 1 只、淀粉 10 克、上浆备用。

②将上过浆的虾仁剁如茸状，放在碗里，加料酒、味精和另一个鸡蛋清搅拌上劲（用力向一个方向搅拌虾茸）后用手捏成直径 25 毫米大的丸子待用。

③将洗净晒干的芝麻粘撒在虾丸子上。

④旺火热锅，放油，待油温升至五成热时，放入虾球炸至金黄色，捞出装盘。

特点：色泽金黄

口味：外脆里嫩

Shrimp Balls with Sesame

Ingredients:

450 grams (0.99 lb) shelled shrimps
50 grams (0.11 lb) white sesame seeds
2 egg whites
5 grams (1 tsp) cooking wine
1 gram (1/4 tsp) MSG
10 grams (1 1/2 tbsp) dry cornstarch
350 grams (1 2/5 cups) oil (only 150 g or 11 tbsp to be consumed)
3 grams (1/2 tsp) salt

Directions:

1. Wash the shrimps clean and drain off the water. Add the salt, 1 egg white and cornstarch for later use.

2. Chop the coated shrimps into paste and place in a bowl. Add the cooking wine, MSG and 1 egg white and stir well in one direction till substance becomes sticky. Shape into balls 2.5 cm (1 inch) in diameter.

3. Dust the shrimp balls with previously washed and dried sesame seeds.

4. Heat the oil to 110-135℃ (230-275℉) and deep-fry the shrimp balls until they are golden in color. Take out and put on a serving plate.

Features: Golden colored.
Taste: Crispy outside and tender inside.

芝麻虾球
Shrimp Balls with Sesame

回锅肉片

主料:带皮猪腿肉 250 克

辅料:大葱 150 克、芹菜 50 克

调料:甜面酱 10 克、料酒 10 克、豆瓣辣酱 25 克、酱油 5 克、白糖 5 克、油 25 克、干红辣椒 2 克

制作:①猪腿肉刮洗干净,放入锅中加水煮至皮软肉熟,捞出冷却。

②冷却后,将猪腿肉切成 5 厘米长、0.3 厘米厚、3 厘米宽的片。大葱剥去黄叶、根、须洗净,斜切成片。芹菜切成段。

③炒锅烧热,倒入油,烧至五成热时,下肉片,煸炒至肉片紧缩卷起,下干红辣椒、豆瓣辣酱、甜面酱、料酒、白糖、酱油、芹菜段翻炒均匀,上色后再投入大葱片翻炒几下,出锅装盘。

特点:色呈酱红

口味:鲜咸甜辣,香味扑鼻

Twice-cooked Pork with Spicy Sauce

Ingredients:

250 grams (0.55 lb) pork leg meat with the skin on
150 grams (0.33 lb) scallions
50 grams (0.11 lb) celery
10 grams (2 tsp) sweet soy bean paste
25 grams (1 tbsp) spicy bean paste
10 grams (2 tsp) cooking wine
5 grams (1 tsp) soy sauce
5 grams (1 tsp) sugar
25 grams (2 tbsp) cooking oil
2 grams (1/15 oz) dry red chili

Directions:

1. Boil the pork leg until the skin becomes soft and the meat is done. Take out and cool off.

2. Cut the meat into slices 5 cm (2 inches) long, 0.3 cm (0.12 inch) thick and 3 cm (1.2 inches) wide. Cut the scallions into slices. Cut the celery into sections 3 cm (1.2 inches) long.

3. Heat the oil to 110-135℃ (230-275˚F). Put in the pork slices and stir-fry until the slices roll up. Put in the red chili, spicy bean paste, sweet bean paste, cooking wine, sugar, soy sauce and celery, and stir well several times. When brown color shows on the meat and celery, add the scallions and keep stirring several more times. Put on a plate and serve.

Features: Dark brown in color.
Taste: Salty, sweet and spicy with a strong delicious aroma.

Twice-Cooked Pork with Green S

葱爆鸭丝

主料：鸭脯肉 250 克

辅料：笋 20 克，葱 50 克

调料：油 500 克（实耗 75 克）、盐 4 克、味精 2 克、料酒 5 克、干淀粉 2 克、清汤 50 克

制作：①将鸭脯肉切成长 5 厘米、宽 0.5 厘米、厚 0.5 厘米的丝。笋切成长 3 厘米、宽 0.3 厘米、厚 0.3 厘米的丝。葱切成 3 厘米的段。盐、味精、料酒、清汤、淀粉放入碗中调合成芡汁。

②炒锅置旺火上烧热，倒入油，烧至五成热时，放入鸭丝滑炒至断生，倒入漏勺中，控净油。

③锅内留余油 25 克烧热，放入葱段、笋丝煸炒出香味，倒入鸭丝及调好的芡汁翻炒均匀，淋上少许麻油，装盘即成。

特点：葱香肉嫩

口味：咸鲜

Quick-fried Shredded Duck with Scallions

Ingredients:

250 grams (0.55 lb) duck breast
20 grams (2/3 oz) bamboo shoots
50 grams (0.11 lb) scallions
500 grams (2 cups) oil (only 75 g or 5 tbsp to be consumed)
4 grams (2/3 tsp) salt
2 grams (1/2 tsp) MSG
5 grams (1 tsp) cooking wine
2 grams (1 tsp) dry cornstarch
50 grams (6 tbsp) water

Directions:

1. Cut the duck breast into shreds 5 cm (2 inches) long and 0.5 cm (0.2 inch) thick and wide. Cut the bamboo shoots into shreds 3 cm (1.2 inches) long and 0.3 cm (0.12 inch) thick and wide. Cut the scallions into sections 3 cm (1.2 inches) long. Put the salt, MSG, cooking wine, water and cornstarch in a bowl to make a paste.

2. Heat the oil in a wok over strong fire to 110-135℃ (230-275˚F) and quickly slippery-fry the duck shreds. Put in a strainer to drain off the oil.

3. Keep 25 g (1 2/3 tbsp) of oil in the wok and put in the scallion and bamboo shreds to stir-fry until they produce a distinctive aroma. Add the duck shreds and the pre-prepared paste to evenly turn several times. Sprinkle on a few drops of sesame oil and it is ready to serve.

Features: The scallion has a strong aroma and the duck meat is tender.
Taste: Salty and delicious.

葱爆鸭丝
Quick-fried Shredded Duck with Scallions

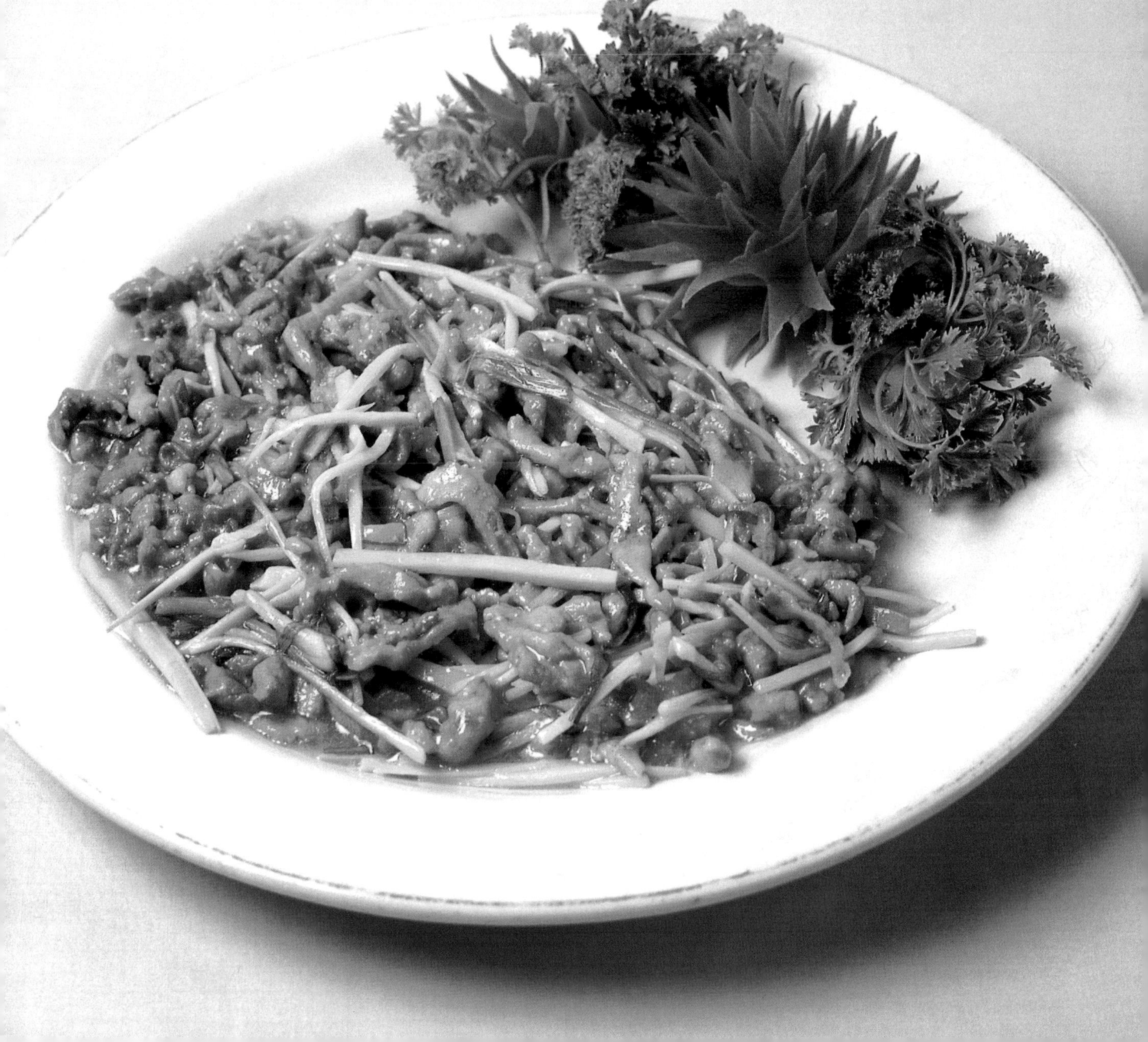

松鼠鱼

主料：鳜鱼1条（约750克）。

辅料：虾仁30克、笋丁20克、水发香菇丁20克、青豌豆15粒（左右）。

调料：料酒20克、盐7克、糖150克、香醋100克、番茄酱100克、淀粉500克（实耗100克左右）、清汤100克、湿淀粉35克、麻油10克、油1000克（实耗200克）。

制作：①鱼洗杀干净，把鱼平放在砧板上，用刀沿胸鳍切下鱼头，从头颈部用刀沿鱼脊背骨两侧剖切至鱼尾（不切断鱼尾），斩去鱼背骨，再用刀沿肋骨侧线平行割去胸刺骨，在两片鱼肉内侧，先纵向直刀，刀距1厘米，再横向划，刀距2厘米，纵横刀深均至皮（不能破皮），成菱形小块，用料酒10克、盐5克，腌渍5分钟，然后在鱼头、鱼肉上拍上淀粉，用手捏住鱼尾，抖去余粉，备用。

②旺火热锅放油，待油温升至八成热时，把刚拍好粉的鱼向内翻卷，鱼皮在里，鱼肉在外，一手持鱼尾，一手用筷子夹住另一端，放入油锅中炸，待成形后松手，放入鱼头同炸至熟，捞出，装在盘中，安上鱼头。

③另取容器放番茄酱、清汤、糖，料酒10克，盐2克，合成卤汁备用。

④锅中留余油20克，放入虾仁，笋丁，水发香菇丁，青豌豆，翻炒至熟后，倒入卤汁，烧沸后用湿淀粉勾芡，淋热麻油出锅，浇在炸好的鳜鱼身上即成。

特点：造型美观，形似松鼠

口味：酸甜可口，外脆里嫩

Sweet and Sour Fish in Squirrel Shape

Ingredients:

1 freshwater fish (preferably mandarin fish) of about 750 grams (1.65lb)

30 grams (1 1/15 oz) shrimps

20 grams (2/3 oz) diced bamboo shoots

20 grams (2/3 oz) diced mushrooms (originally dried mushrooms that have been soaked in water)

15 grams (1/2 oz) green peas

20 grams (4 tsp) cooking wine

7 grams (1 1/6 tsp) salt

150 grams (11 tbsp) sugar

100 grams (6 tbsp) vinegar

100 grams (5 1/2 tbsp) tomato sauce

500 grams (1.1lb) dry cornstarch (only about 100 g or 0.22lb to be used)

100 grams (6tbsp) water

35 grams (2tbsp) mixture of cornstarch and water

10 grams (2tsp) sesame oil

1,000 grams (4cups) oil (200g or 4/5cup to be consumed)

Directions:

1. Clean the fish, cut off the head near the belly fin, but do not throw it away. Cut open the fish along its back until the cut reaches its tail. (Do not cut off the tail.) Cut out the back bone and remove the side bones (ribs). Make several cuts with 1 cm spaces in between, first vertically and then horizontally on the inner side of the fish to create a diamond-shaped pattern. (Do not cut open the skin.) Marinate the fish with 10g (2tsp) of cooking wine and 5g (5/6tsp) of salt for 5 minutes. Dust the dry cornstarch on the fish body and head. Hold the fish tail to shake off unnecessary cornstarch.

2. Heat the oil until it is about 200-220℃ (390-430℉). Roll the fish to keep the skin inside. Hold the fish tail with one hand and the top end of the fish body with chopsticks and gradually release it into the oil. Now place the head into the oil also. When both are done, take them out and place them on a plate, putting the head and the body together to create the concept of a whole fish.

3. Mix the tomato sauce, water, sugar, 10 g (2tsp) of cooking wine and 2 g (1/3tsp) of salt into a sauce.

4. Keep 20g (1 1/2tbsp) of oil in the wok. Put in the shrimps, diced bamboo shoots, mushrooms and green peas and stir-fry. Add in the mixed sauce. When the sauce is boiling, put in the cornstarch-water mixture to thicken it. Sprinkle some sesame oil and pour the sauce right onto the fish.

Features: It beautifully resembles the shape of a squirrel.

Taste: Both sweet and sour, crispy outside and tender inside.

松鼠鱼
Sweet and Sour Fish in Squirrel Shape

什锦素菜包

主料：胡萝卜 20 克、水发香菇 20 克、火腿 20 克、笋 20 克

辅料：生菜 30 克

调料：盐 1 克、糖 2 克、酱油 2 克、色拉油 10 克、味精 1 克

制作：①将胡萝卜、香菇、火腿、笋切成碎丁，加盐、糖、酱油、味精炒熟待用。

②将生菜洗净，放入开水锅中焯一下，捞出，把菜叶切成长 8 厘米、宽 5 厘米的长方形待用。

③将切好的生菜叶平放在砧板上，放上馅，包成 3 厘米宽的长条形，码入盘中，上笼蒸 5 分钟即可。

特点：色泽美观，爽脆鲜美

口味：咸鲜

Assorted Vegetables Wrapped in Lettuce

Ingredients：

20 grams (2/3 oz) carrots
20 grams (2/3 oz) mushrooms
20 grams (2/3 oz) ham
20 grams (2/3 oz) bamboo shoots
30 grams (1 oz) lettuce
1 gram (1/6 tsp) salt
2 grams (1/2 tsp) sugar
2 grams (1/2 tsp) soy sauce
10 grams (1 1/2 tsp) salad oil
1 gram (1/4 tsp) MSG

Directions：

1. Cut carrots, mushrooms, and ham into small cubes. Add the salt, sugar, soy sauce and MSG and stir-fry. Put aside.

2. Quickly boil the lettuce. Take it out and cut into rectangles 8 cm (3.2 inches) long and 5 cm (2 inches) wide.

3. Place the lettuce rectangles flat on a chopping board. Put the mixture of vegetables and ham on the lettuce as filling. Fold into rectangles 3 cm (1.2 inches) wide. Place on a plate and steam for 5 minutes.

Features：Beautiful in color and looks very fresh.
Taste：Salty and delicious.

什锦素菜包

Assorted Vegetables Wrapped in Lettuce

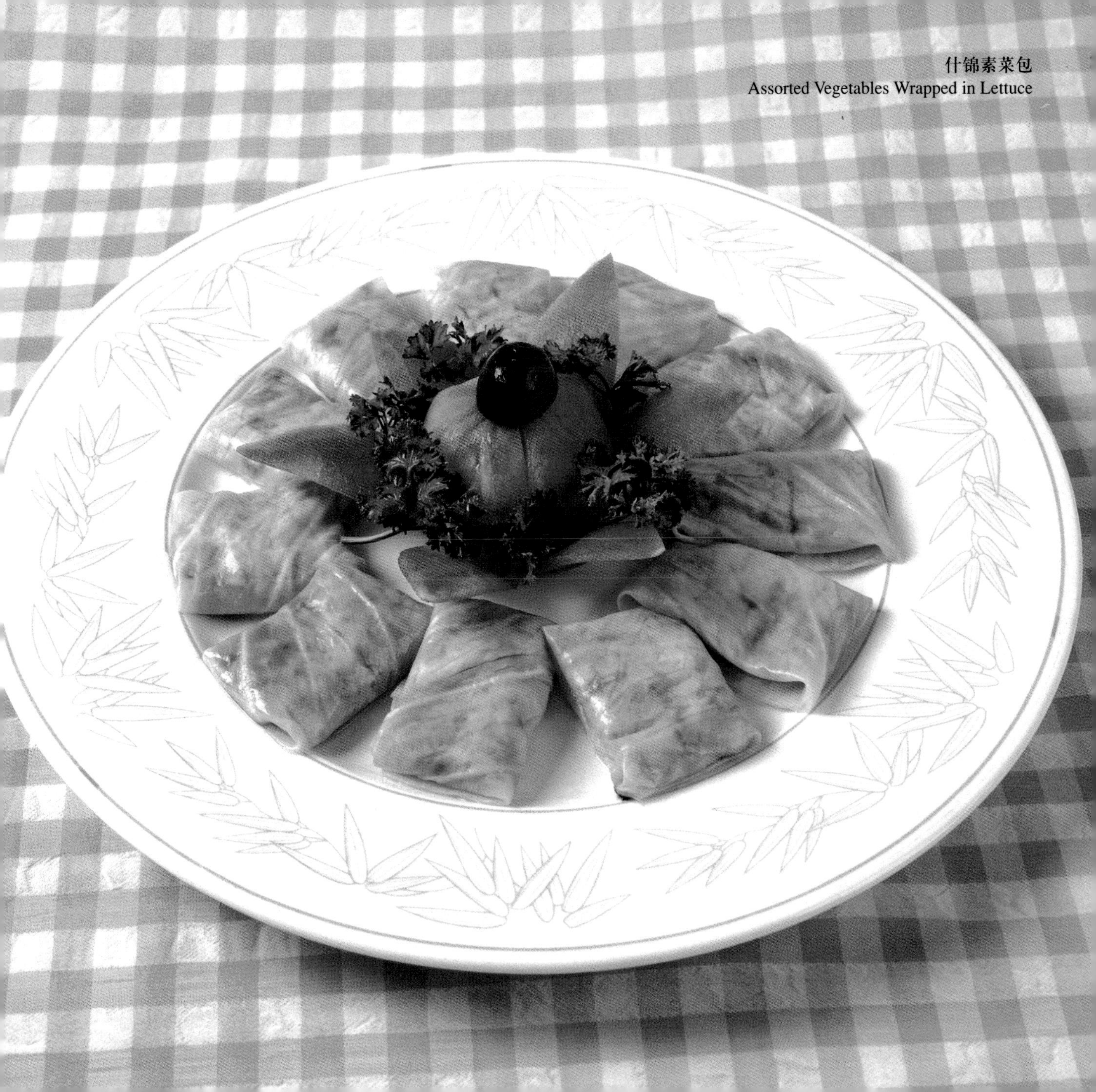

淀粉虾饺

主料：淀粉 500 克

辅料：糯米粉 100 克、虾仁 250 克、笋丝 50 克、胡萝卜丝 50 克、猪肥膘 100 克。

调料：盐 3 克、糖 1 克、味精 1 克、料酒 10 克、葱花 5 克、熟猪油 50 克。

制法：①虾仁、笋丝、胡萝卜丝、肥膘洗净剁碎，加入盐、味精、料酒、葱花，拌匀用作馅心。

②淀粉、糯粉、熟猪油拌匀，加入 150 克开水搅拌成粉团，揉透，摘成每只 20 克的坯子，用手再将坯子撅扁、压薄使之成为圆形皮子。皮子中间放上馅心，对折成半圆形，沿边推捏成花边，上笼，待水沸后，大火蒸 10 分钟即可。

特点：色泽洁白，形态美观

口味：咸鲜

Steamed Dumpling with Shrimp

Ingredients：
500 grams (1.1 lb) cornstarch
100 grams (0.22 lb) glutinous rice flour
250 grams (0.55 lb) shelled shrimps
50 grams (0.11 lb) shredded bamboo shoots
50 grams (0.11 lb) shredded carrots
100 grams (0.22 lb) pork fat
3 grams (1/2 tsp) salt
1 gram (1/4 tsp) sugar
1 gram (1/4 tsp) MSG
10 grams (2 tsp) cooking wine
5 grams (1/6 oz) finely cut scallions
50 grams (0.11 lb) lard

Directions：

1. Wash clean and finely chop the shelled shrimps, bamboo shoots, shredded carrots and pork fat. Add the salt, MSG, cooking wine and scallions to make the filling.

2. Mix the cornstarch, rice flour with the lard. Add 150 g (10 tbsp) of boiling water and mix well. Divide into small pieces each 20 g (2/3 oz) in weight. Press them into flat wrappings by hand, put in the filling and seal well. Put them in a steamer and when the water starts to boil, steam them for 10 minutes. Now serve.

Features：Pure white in color and beautiful in shape.
Taste： Salty and tasty.

淀粉虾饺
Steamed Dumpling with Shrimp

花篮烧麦

主料：面粉 250 克、肉末 200 克

辅料：蔬菜叶 20 克

调料：盐 5 克、糖 15 克、味精 2 克、葱姜各 5 克

制法：①肉末加盐、糖、味精、葱姜拌匀后加入 50 克水，顺一个方向搅拌，直至有韧劲，馅心待用。

②面粉加 80 克开水和成面团，待凉后，揉透搓条，再摘成每只 15 克的坯子，压扁后用面棍制成直径 10cm 的圆皮备用。

③圆面皮上包入馅心用手指在皮子中部微微收紧，使上部皮子收口处成开花状，再取少许面团加蔬菜汁揉匀，搓成细条装饰，将生坯上笼蒸十分种即可。

特点：形状逼真，色泽鲜艳

口味：咸鲜

Flowery Steamed Dumpling

Ingredients:

250 grams (0.55 lb) wheat flour
200 grams (0.44 lb) minced meat
20 grams (2/3 oz) green vegetable juice
5 grams (5/6 tsp) salt
15 grams (1 tbsp) sugar
2 grams (1/2 tsp) MSG
5 grams (1/6 oz) scallions
5 grams (1/6 oz) ginger

Directions:

1. Add the salt, sugar, MSG, and chopped scallions and ginger to the minced meat, put in 50 g (3 tbsp) of water and well stir in one direction till it becomes sticky.

2. Add 80 g (5 tbsp) of hot water to the flour to make dough. When it cools off, roll the dough well and then divide into pieces 15 g (1/2 oz) each in weight. Press with a roller into round flat wrappings 10 cm (4 inches) in diameter.

3. Put the mixture of meat in the middle of each wrapping and carefully fold. Leave the top of each dumpling open in a shape of a flower. Mix green vegetable juice with a small amount of the dough and roll into green-colored thick threads to decorate the dumplings with patterns desired by the cook. Steam for 10 minutes and the dumplings are ready to serve.

Features: In beautiful colors, the dumplings look vividly like blossoming flowers.

Taste: Salty and delicious.

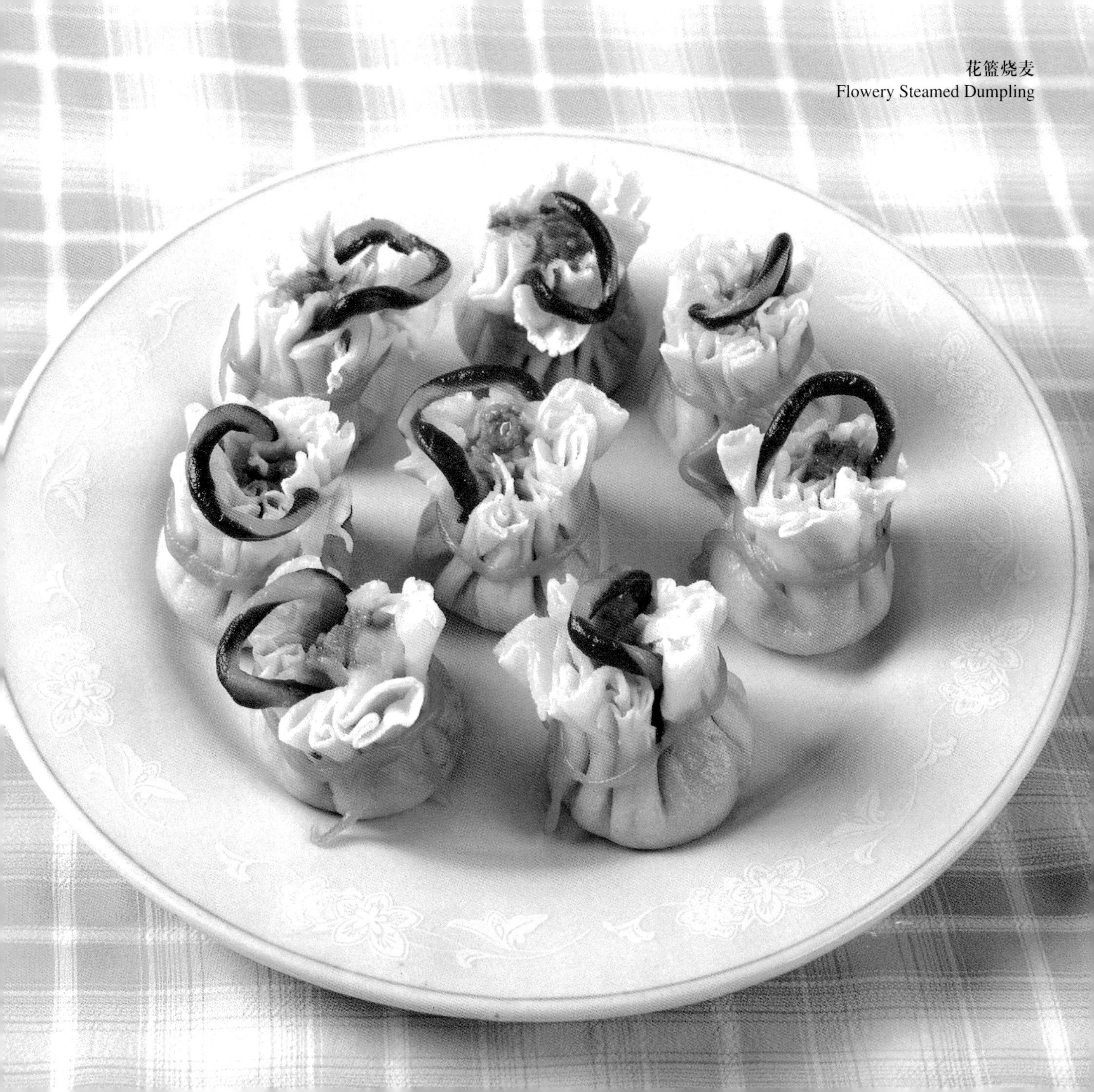

花篮烧麦
Flowery Steamed Dumpling

六生火锅

主料：生鸡胸脯肉 150 克、生牛肉 100 克、生鱼肉 100 克、生虾仁 100 克、生猪肉 100 克、生鲜贝 100 克

辅料：时令蔬菜等（青菜、粉丝、豆腐、生菜、百叶结、白菜各 100 克）

调料：红辣椒 10 只、盐 3 克、味精 2 克、葱姜各 5 克、油 50 克、鸡汤 1000 克、海米 15 克；花生酱、酱油、麻油、番茄酱、辣椒酱、韭菜花、甜面酱若干

制作：①将主料（除虾仁、鲜贝）分别切成长约 5 厘米、宽约 1.5 厘米的薄片（越薄越好），装在盘中，蔬菜分别加工洗净装盘，将花生酱等按各自口味调好装在小碗里以备蘸食。

②锅放火上烧热放入油、红辣椒翻炒后加鸡汤、盐、葱姜、味精、海米煮沸后，倒入火锅中放在便炉上边烧边涮肉、海鲜、蔬菜等，涮好后可根据各自口味蘸调料食用。

特点：现涮现吃

口味：鲜辣

Six-meat Hotpot

Ingredients：

150 grams (0.33 lb) chicken breast
100 grams (0.22 lb) tender beef
100 grams (0.22 lb) fish meat
100 grams (0.22 lb) shelled shrimp
100 grams (0.22 lb) pork
100 grams (0.22 lb) fresh scallops
100 grams (0.22 lb) green vegetable
100 grams (0.22 lb) bean threads
100 grams (0.22 lb) bean curd
100 grams (0.22 lb) lettuce
100 grams (0.22 lb) Chinese cabbage
10 pieces red chili
3 grams (1/2 tsp) salt
2 grams (1/2 tsp) MSG
5 grams (1/6 oz) finely cut scallions
5 grams (1/6 oz) ginger shreds
1,000 grams (4 cups) chicken soup
15 grams (1/2 oz) dried shrimp
50 grams (3 tbsp) cooking oil
Peanut butter
Soy sauce
Sesame oil
Ketchup
Chili paste
Sweet bean paste
Pickled leek flowers

Directions：

1. Cut the meat, except for shrimps and scallops, into slices 5 cm (2 inches) long, 1.5 cm (0.6 inch) wide and as thin as possible. Place on plates. Wash the vegetables and put on plates. Into serving bowls, according to each one's own taste, mix peanut butter and other seasonings.

2. Heat the oil in a wok and stir-fry the red chili. Add the chicken soup, salt, scallions, ginger, MSG and dried shrimp, and bring to a boil. Pour the soup into a pot and keep heating it. Dip the meat, vegetables, bean curd and bean threads bit by bit into the soup pot and then dip in one's own sauce.

Features: This is a dish that people enjoy eating while it cooks.

Taste: Very delicious with a spicy touch.

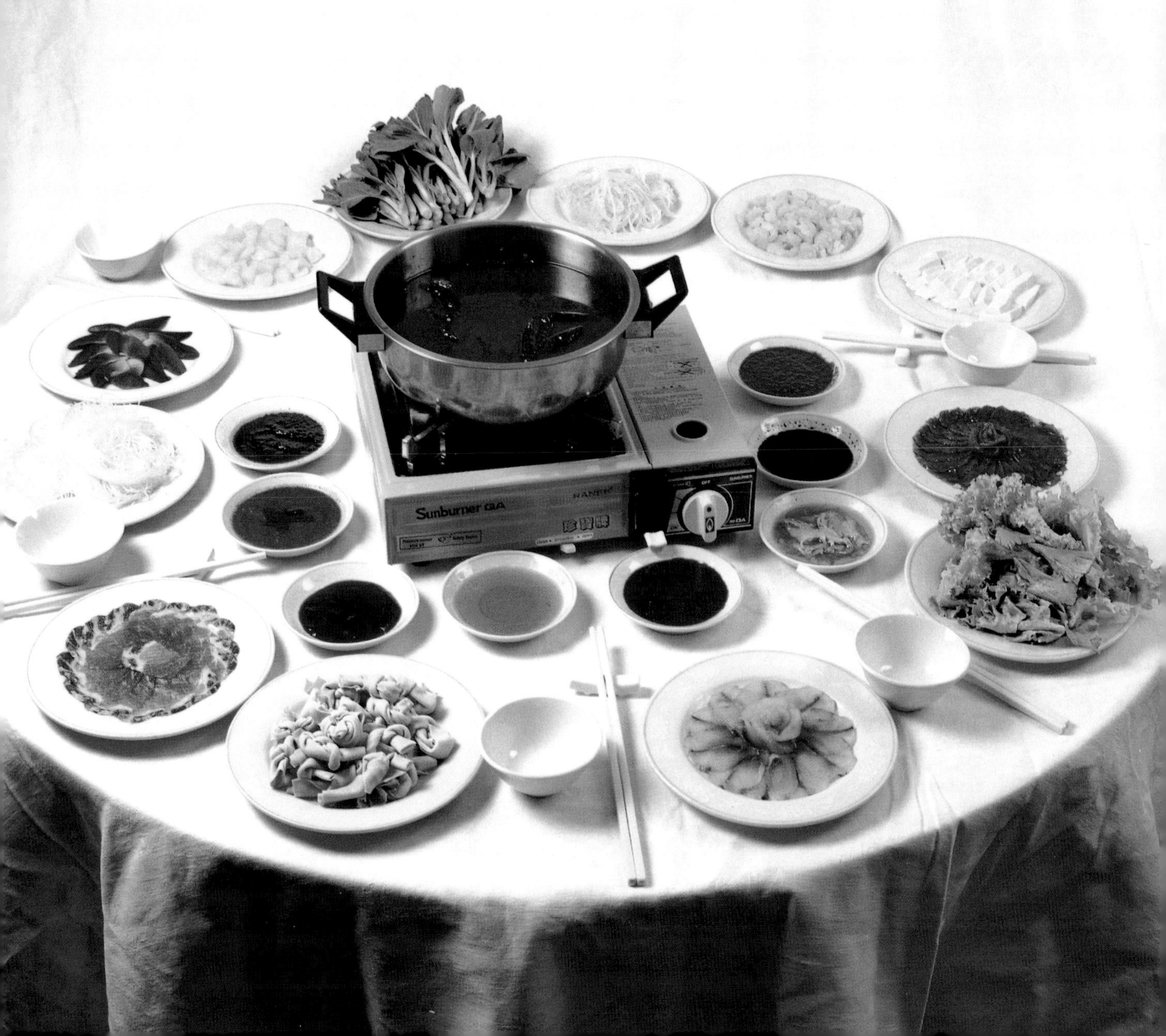

六生火锅
Six-meat Hotpot

5-7人宴席(A)

第一道菜：六味冷碟

第二道菜：白灼基围虾

第三道菜：松仁玉米

第四道菜：荷叶粉蒸肉

第五道菜：西瓜鸡

第六道菜：炒素什锦

第七道菜：火腿桂鱼

第八道菜：花色蒸饺

主　　食：开花馒头

　　汤：　鸳鸯莼菜汤

六味冷碟

麻油苦瓜，盐水牛肉，金丝瓜，白斩鸡，凉拌葱油海蜇，
咸菜毛豆

Family Feast for 5 to 7 People

（Type A)

Course 1：Six Cold Dishes

Course 2：Boiled Shrimp

Course 3：Pine Nuts with Sweet Corn

Course 4：Pork and Rice Wrapped with Lotus Leaves

Course 5：Tender Chicken in Watermelon

Course 6：Mixed Vegetables

Course 7：Mandarin Fish with Ham

Course 8：Steamed Dumpling in Flower Shape

Staple Food：Flowery Steamed Bun

Soup：Mandarin Duck and Water Shield Soup

Six Cold Dishes

Balsam Pear with Sesame Oil, Salted Beef Slices, Wax Gourd with Lemon Juice, Soy Tender Chicken, Shredded Jelly Fish with Scallion Oil and Salted Tender Soy Beans

六味冷碟
Six Cold Dishes

白灼基围虾

主料：活基围虾 500 克

辅料：清水 1500 克

调料：料酒 10 克、葱段姜片各 5 克、味精 1 克、胡椒粉 0.5 克、酱油 25 克、香醋 5 克

制作：①将基围虾洗净滤干水份备用，酱油、味精、胡椒粉、醋调拌好装在碟中。

②炒锅加清水烧开，将虾倒入锅中加料酒、葱段、姜片烧至壳红、肉质饱满即捞出装盘上桌，就调味品蘸食。

注：因各国人的口味不一样，调料可根据各自的口味调配，可用番茄酱加果汁调成果汁味，橙汁加蚝油也可。

特点：制作简单

口味：基围虾肉质鲜、香

Boiled Shrimp

Ingredients：
500 grams (1.1 lb) live freshwater shrimps
1,500 grams (6 cups) water
10 grams (2 tsp) cooking wine
5 grams (1/6 oz) sectioned scallions
5 grams (1/6 oz) chopped ginger
1 gram (1/4 tsp) MSG
1/2 gram (1/10 tsp) pepper powder
25 grams (1 1/2 tbsp) soy sauce
5 grams (1 tsp) vinegar

Directions：
1. Wash the shrimps clean for later use.

2. Bring the water to a boil, put in the live shrimps and add the cooking wine, scallions and ginger, and cook until the shrimps turn red and fill up their shells. Take out and put on a plate. Serve by dipping into the sauce.

3. Put the soy sauce, MSG, pepper powder and vinegar on a plate and mix to make a sauce. (Ketchup and fruit juice can also be used to make a fruit-flavored sauce. Alternatively orange juice and oyster sauce can be used to make another type of sauce.)

Features：Easy to cook.
Taste：The shrimps taste very tender and delicious.

白灼基围虾
Boiled Shrimp

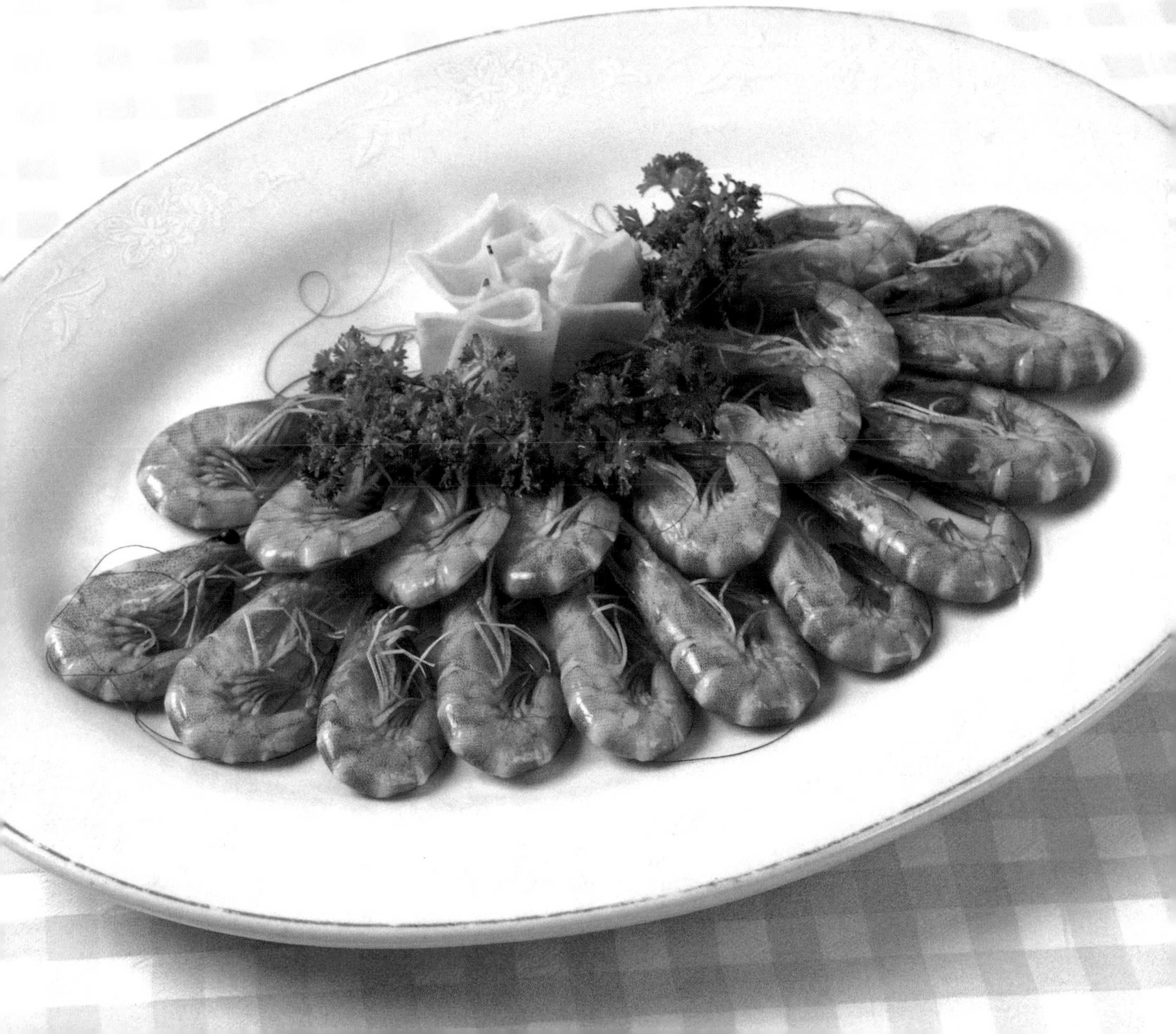

松仁玉米

主料：松仁 50 克、甜玉米粒 350 克

辅料：胡萝卜 150 克、黄瓜 150 克

调料：盐 1 克、味精 1 克、糖 2 克、黄酒 10 克、色拉油 300 克（实耗 60 克）、湿淀粉 15 克、清汤 20 克

制作：①炒锅置火上倒入油，待油温升至五成热时，倒入松仁炸至金黄色，倒入漏勺中滤油。

②胡萝卜、黄瓜洗净，切成 0.3 厘米见方的丁。

③炒锅倒入色拉油 50 克烧热，倒入胡萝卜丁、黄瓜丁煸炒几下后倒入玉米粒，加清汤、盐、味精、料酒烧沸后倒入松仁，用湿淀粉勾芡，迅速出锅装盘即可。

特点：青黄红相间

口味：咸鲜清香

Pine Nuts with Sweet Corn

Ingredients：

50 grams (0.11 lb) shelled pine nuts
350 grams (0.77 lb) sweet corn grains
50 grams (0.11 lb) carrots
150 grams (0.33 lb) cucumbers
1 gram (1/6 tsp) salt
1 gram (1/4 tsp) MSG
2 grams (1/2 tsp) sugar
10 grams (2 tsp) cooking wine
300 grams (1 2/5 cups) salad oil (only 1/5 to be consumed)
15 grams (1 tbsp) mixture of cornstarch and water
20 grams (1 1/2 tbsp) water

Directions：

1. Heat oil to 110-135℃ (230-275℉) and put in the pine nuts to deep-fry until they are golden yellow. Take out and drain off the oil.

2. Wash clean the carrots and cucumbers and cut into cubes 0.3 cm (0.12 in) each side.

3. Put 50 g (3 1/2 tbsp) of salad oil back in the wok, heat it and put in the carrot and cucumber cubes to stir-fry. Add the sweet corn, water, salt, MSG and cooking wine. Bring these ingredients to boil and then put in the pine nuts. Use mixture of cornstarch and water to thicken the soup and quickly put on a plate to serve.

Features：Beautifully combined colors of yellow and green.
Taste：Salty, refreshing and fragrant.

松仁玉米
Pine Nuts with Sweet Corn

荷叶粉蒸肉

主料：猪硬肋肉（俗称五花肉）600 克

辅料：荷叶 3 张、粳米 150 克

调料：甜面酱 40 克、葱段 25 克、姜片 25 克、料酒 35 克、酱油 60 克、味精 3 克、糖 20 克、丁香 2 克、茴香 2 克、桂皮 2 克

制作：①将粳米洗净滤干，与丁香桂皮、茴香一起放在炒锅内小火炒至米呈金黄色香气扑鼻倒出冷却，后除去桂皮、丁香、茴香并用粉碎机加工成米粉备用。

②猪五花肉刮去细毛剔去肋骨洗净，切成长 15 厘米、宽 2 厘米、厚 1 厘米的片。放姜、葱、料酒、酱油、糖、甜面酱、味精拌匀后腌渍一小时。

③把腌渍过的肉同米粉拌和，荷叶裁切，热水洗烫后逐块包肉，放在笼屉上旺火蒸两小时即可。

特点：清香扑鼻

口味：酥烂不腻

Pork and Rice Wrapped with Lotus Leaves

Ingredients：

600 grams (1.2 lb) streaky pork
3 pieces of lotus leaves
150 grams (0.33 lb) round-grained non-glutinous rice
40 grams (2 1/4 tbsp) sweet bean paste
25 grams (5/6 oz) sectioned scallions
25 grams (5/6 oz) sliced ginger
35 grams (2 1/2 tbsp) cooking wine
60 grams (3 tbsp) soy sauce
3 grams (3/4 tsp) MSG
20 grams (1 1/2 tbsp) sugar
2 grams (1/15 oz) dry clove
2 grams (1/15 oz) aniseed
2 grams (1/15 oz) cinnamon

Directions：

1. Get rid of all the bones and hair from the pork. Cut into slices 15 cm (6 inches) long, 2 cm (0.8 inch) wide and 1 cm (0.4 inch) thick. Marinate for 1 hour with ginger, scallions, cooking wine, soy sauce, sugar, sweet bean paste and MSG.

2. Wash the non-glutinous rice and drain off the water. Bake the rice over a low fire together with dry clove, aniseed and cinnamon until the rice becomes yellowish in color and produces a strong fragrance. Remove the spices and grind the rice into flour.

3. Mix the rice flour with the marinated pork. Cut the lotus leaves into smaller pieces, wash with hot water and wrap the meat piece by piece. Steam over a strong fire for 2 hours.

Features：Strongly fragrant and inviting.
Taste：Soft, rich but not greasy.

荷叶粉蒸肉
Pork and Rice Wrapped with Lotus Leaves

西瓜鸡

主料：西瓜一只、童仔鸡1只

辅料：火腿50克、笋50克

调料：料酒6克、盐4克、味精1克、鸡汤750克、葱段2克、姜片3克、油5克

制作：①将西瓜洗净，削下顶部做盖，掏净瓜瓤（瓜瓤可作饭后的一道水果），将顶盖和开口处雕成相吻合的齿轮形状，在瓜体外雕上些图案，抹上油备用。

②鸡宰杀去毛、内脏，洗净；火腿、笋切片，同洗净的鸡一起放入汤碗中，加鸡汤、盐、味精、料酒、葱段、姜片，上笼蒸1小时左右。

③将蒸熟的鸡捞去葱姜倒入西瓜盅内，盖上盖再上笼蒸2分钟即可。

特点：造型美观

口味：鸡嫩汤鲜

Tender Chicken in Watermelon

Ingredients：

1 watermelon
1 tender chicken
50 grams (0.11 lb) ham
50 grams (0.11 lb) bamboo shoots
6 grams (1 1/5 tsp) cooking wine
4 grams (2/3 tsp) salt
1 gram (1/4 tsp) MSG
750 grams (3 cups) chicken soup
2 grams (1/15 oz) sectioned scallions
3 grams (1/10 oz) sliced ginger
5 grams (1 tsp) cooking oil

Directions：

1. Wash the watermelon and cut off the top to serve as cover. Remove all the insides which can serve as fruit after dinner. Make saw-teeth shaped cuts around the cover edge and main body edge of the watermelon so that the cover will shut nice and tight. Carve patterns into the outside body of the melon. Rub the melon with oil and put aside for later use.

2. Dress the chicken. Cut the ham and bamboo shoots into slices. Put the slices and the chicken in a soup bowl. Add the chicken soup, salt, MSG, cooking wine, scallions and ginger, and steam for 1 hour.

3. Remove the scallions and ginger from the chicken soup. Put the chicken into the watermelon. Cover and steam for 2 more minutes. It is now ready to serve.

Features：Beautifully shaped.
Taste：The chicken is very tender and the soup delicious.

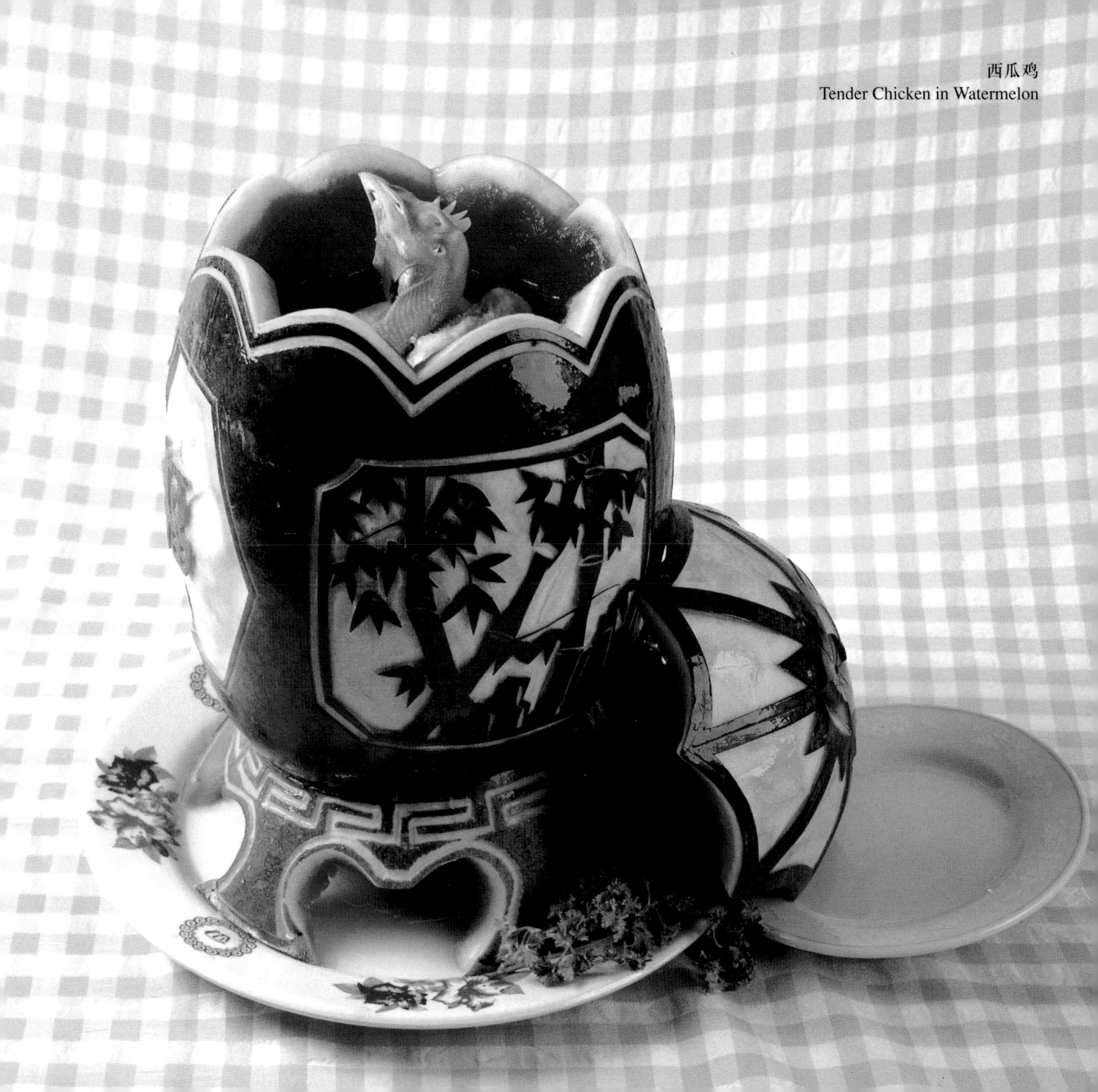

西瓜鸡
Tender Chicken in Watermelon

炒素什锦

主料：胡萝卜 150 克、青椒 150 克、水发香菇 150 克、笋 120 克、油面筋 150 克、荷兰豆 120 克

调料：色拉油 100 克、盐 2 克、料酒 10 克、味精 1 克、湿淀粉 15 克

制作：①将洗净的胡萝卜、青椒（去蒂籽）、香菇、笋、土豆（去皮）、荷兰豆均切成片。油面筋用开水泡一下。

②炒锅烧热倒入色拉油，待油温升至六成热时，倒入土豆片炒至断生后再倒入胡萝卜、青椒、香菇、笋、荷兰豆、油面筋，加盐、料酒、味精翻炒均匀，用湿淀粉勾芡，出锅装盘即成。

特点：颜色鲜艳

口味：咸鲜爽脆

Mixed Vegetables

Ingredients：
150 grams (0.33 lb) carrots
150 grams (0.33 lb) green peppers
150 grams (0.33 lb) mushrooms
120 grams (0.26 lb) bamboo shoots
150 grams (0.33 lb) fried gluten
120 grams (0.26 lb) snow peas
100 grams (7 tbsp) salad oil
2 grams (1/3 tsp) salt
10 grams (2 tsp) cooking wine
1 gram (1/4 tsp) MSG
15 grams (3 tsp) mixture of cornstarch and water

Directions：

1. Cut the carrots, green peppers (with seeds removed), mushrooms, bamboo shoots, potatoes (with skin removed) and snow peas into slices. Quickly soak the fried gluten in hot water.

2. Heat the salad oil to 135-170℃ (275-340℉). Put in the potato slices and stir-fry. Add the carrots, green peppers, mushrooms, bamboo shoots, snow peas, fried gluten, salt, cooking wine, and MSG and stir in the wok. Add the mixture of cornstarch and water. Remove onto a plate and serve.

Features：Beautiful in colors.
Taste：Salty, delicious and crispy.

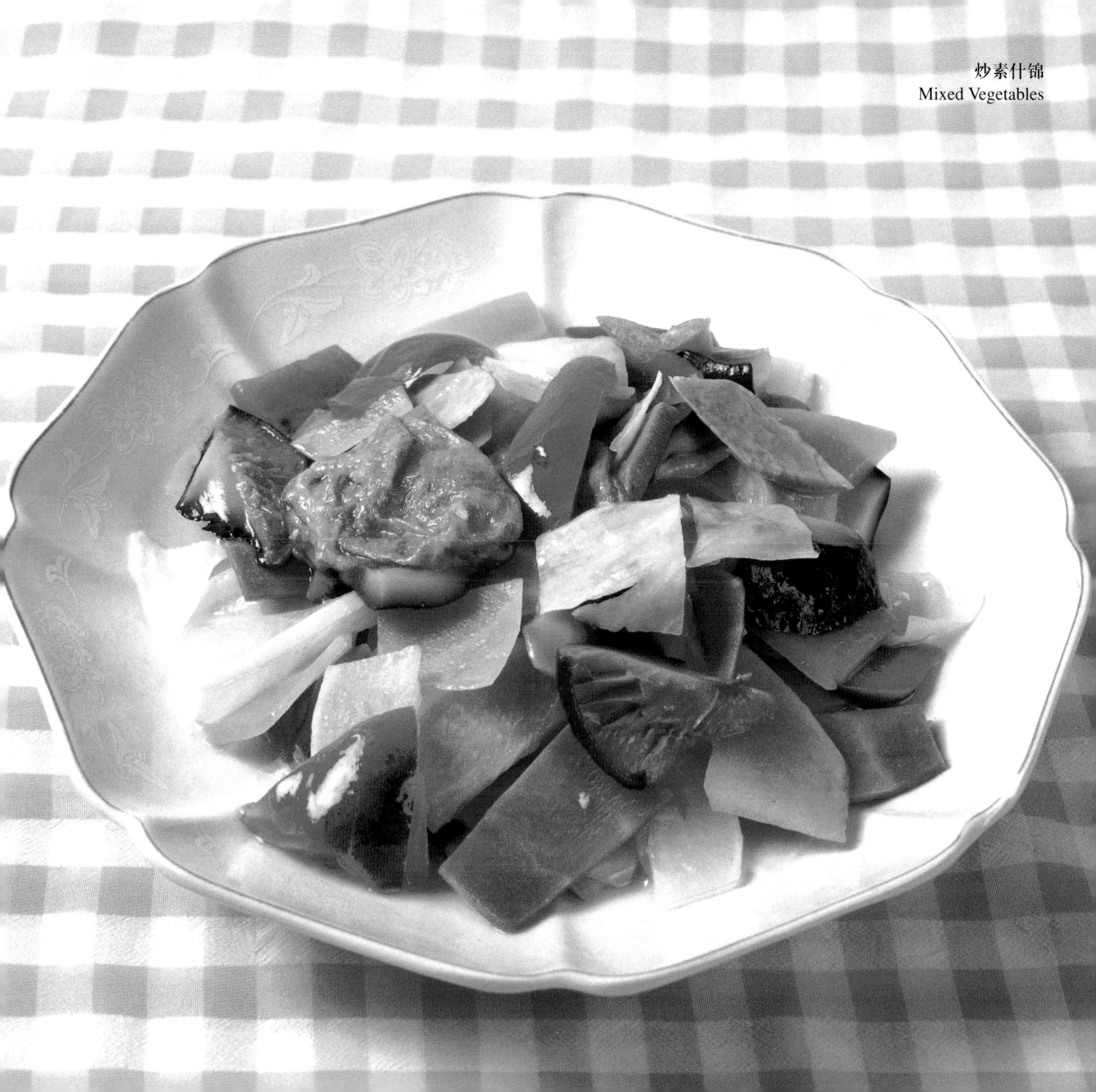

炒素什锦
Mixed Vegetables

火腿桂鱼

主料：750 克左右鲜桂鱼一条

辅料：火腿 50 克、笋（新鲜、罐装均可）50 克

调料：盐 2 克、味精 1 克、料酒 10 克、油 50 克，葱段 5 克，姜片 5 克

制作：①将桂鱼洗杀干净，将头切下，用刀将鱼头下颏处剖开，使脑背部相连，用刀轻轻拍平。用刀从头颈贴鱼背背骨两侧横切至鱼尾，用力在鱼尾部斩断鱼背骨，再用刀贴着两片鱼的肋骨侧线，割下鱼肋骨，然后再在相连两片鱼内上分别横切五刀，注意鱼皮不能破。用清水洗净滤干，撒上盐、味精、料酒腌渍 10 分钟。

②将火腿、笋分别切十片，然后 1 片火腿叠 1 片笋夹在鱼肉中。鱼皮向下放在盘中，前放上鱼头，淋油，放葱段、姜片大火上笼蒸 10 分钟取下，拣去葱姜即可。

特点：形状美观

口味：鱼肉鲜嫩、洁白

Mandarin Fish with Ham

Ingredients：

1 mandarin fish weighing about 750 grams (1.65 lb)

50 grams (0.11 lb) ham

50 grams (0.11 lb) bamboo shoots (fresh or canned)

2 grams (1/3 tsp) salt

1 gram (1/4 tsp) MSG

10 grams (2 tsp) cooking wine

50 grams (3 1/2 tbsp) cooking oil

5 grams (1/6 oz) sectioned scallions

5 grams (1/6 oz) sliced ginger

Directions：

1. Cut the fish head open from the jaw while leaving the skull intact. Lightly press it flat with a cutter. Cut from the back of the head all the way to the tail on both sides of the backbone. Break the backbone at the tail point. Use cutter to remove the ribs. Now make five horizontal cuts on the inside of the fish meat. Make sure not to cut the skin. Wash clean, dust with salt and MSG, and marinate with the cooking wine for 10 minutes.

2. Cut the ham and bamboo shoots into ten slices. Insert a slice of ham and a slice of bamboo at every cut on the fish. Place the fish on a plate with the skin side down. Position the head, sprinkle the oil, add scallions and ginger and heat over a strong fire for 10 minutes. Remove the ginger and scallions and serve.

Features：The cooked fish looks inviting.

Taste：The meat is white and tender.

火腿桂鱼
Mandarin Fish with Ham

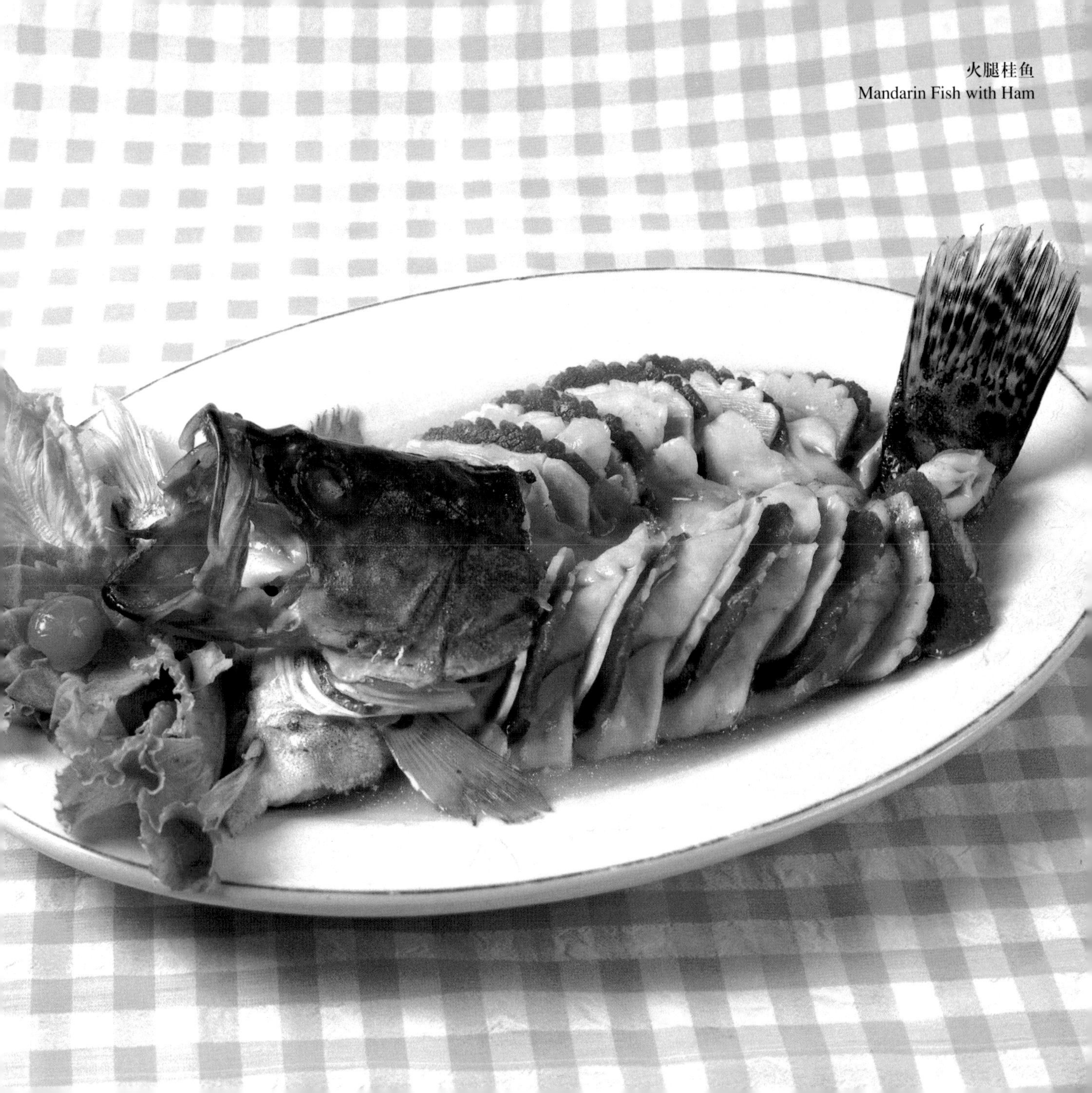

花色蒸饺

主料：面粉 200 克、肉末 200 克

辅料：青菜汁 20 克

调料：盐 3 克、糖 6 克、味精 2 克、料酒 5 克、葱姜末各 2 克

制法：①将肉末加盐、糖、味精、料酒、葱姜拌匀后，加 50 克水，顺一个方向用力搅拌直至肉馅有韧劲。

②面粉加开水拌成粉团，揉透，搓成圆形长条，按每只 15 克摘坯，将坯压扁用面棍制成薄圆面皮。

③面皮包入馅，按 5 等份捏起收口，再将每条边用手指捏出各种各样形状，在花边上涂上青菜汁上笼蒸 10 分钟即可。

特点：形象美观

口味：咸鲜

Steamed Dumpling in Flower Shape

Ingredients：

200 grams (0.44 lb) wheat flour
200 grams (0.44 lb) minced meat
20 grams (1 1/2 tbsp) green vegetable juice
3 grams (1/2 tsp) salt
6 grams (1 1/5 tsp) sugar
2 grams (1/2 tsp) MSG
5 grams (1 tsp) cooking wine
2 grams (1/15 oz) finely cut scallions
2 grams (1/15 oz) chopped ginger

Directions：

1. Add the salt, sugar, MSG, cooking wine, scallions and ginger to the minced meat and mix well. Add 50 g (3 tbsp) of water and stir in one direction till substance becomes sticky.

2. Use hot water to mix the flour to produce dough. Mix well and shape into a long roll. Divide the dough into small pieces 15 g (1/2 oz) each in weight. Press with a roller to make thin wrappings.

3. Put some of the mixture of meat on each wrapping, fold up in five equal sections so that the folds at the top of the dumpling appear to consist of five parts. Make nice-looking shapes at the end of the folds. Apply some green vegetable juice on the folds to add color. Steam for 10 minutes and the dumplings are ready to serve.

Features：Beautifully shaped.
Taste：Salty and delicious.

花色蒸饺
Steamed Dumpling in Flower Shape

开花馒头

主料：面粉 500 克

辅料：糖 150 克、鲜酵母 20 克、猪板油 100 克

调料：糖桂花 5 克

制法：①面粉加鲜酵母拌匀，加入 200 克温水和成面团，静置 1 小时。

②将猪板油切丁和糖、糖桂花一起，剁成泥状。也可用粉碎机粉碎。

③将发好的面团揉透，搓成直径 5 厘米的圆长条，用刀在长条两边划开两条深沟，填入搓成细长条的猪板油，虽后将开口处捏拢。将长条摘成每只 20 克的坯，直接放在笼上，沸水旺火蒸 25 分钟即可。

特点：松软

口味：香甜

Flowery Steamed Bun

Ingredients：

500 grams (1.1 lb) wheat flour
150 grams (0.33 lb) sugar
20 grams (2/3 oz) yeast (optional)
100 grams (0.22 lb) pork fat
5 grams (1 tsp) sweetened osmanthus sauce

Directions：

1. Mix the yeast with the flour or use self-rising flour. Use 200 g (2/5 cup) of lukewarm water to turn the flour into dough and put aside for an hour.

2. Cut the pork fat into small cubes and mix with sugar and osmanthus syrup. Chop the mixture into paste or make paste with a grinder.

3. Mix well and press the dough and make a long strip 5 cm (slightly under 2 inches) in diameter. Make two deep cuts with a knife on both sides of the long strip of dough and fill up the cuts with the paste. Reduce the dough into small pieces each weighing about 20 g (2/3 oz). Place them on the tray of a steamer.

4. Put 2,500 g (10 cups) of water in the steamer and bring it to boil. Put the tray with the buns into the steamer and cook over high heat for 25 minutes and they are ready to eat.

Features：They have a beautiful appearance as the top shows a flower-like opening and are soft to the taste.

Taste：Fragrant and sweet.

开花馒头
Flowery Steamed Bun

鸳鸯莼菜汤

主料：莼菜 150 克（莼菜：水生宿根草本，性喜温暖，江南地区多野生并以太湖莼菜最为有名）

辅料：火腿 20 克、鸡蛋清 2 只、胡萝卜 4 克、黑芝麻 4 粒

调料：盐 3 克、味精 1 克、胡椒粉 0.5 克、油 5 克、鸡汤 500 克

制作：①将火腿切成薄片，鸡蛋清放在碗里用打蛋器顺一个方向搅拌，搅到形成雪白有浓稠的泡沫，筷子戳在其中立着不倒为好。

②小匙抹上油放上打好的鸡蛋清，用餐刀将鸡蛋清塑成鸳鸯，胡萝卜切成薄片用小刀刻成翅膀形状按在鸡蛋清塑成的鸳鸯身上，黑芝麻点做眼睛，之后上笼蒸，上气后 1—2 秒钟取下备用。

③锅放在火上，放入约 1500 克清水，烧沸后将莼菜倒入焯水（目的是使莼菜碧绿），倒出滤干后放入汤碗中。

④锅放在火上倒入鸡汤，放入火腿、盐、味精烧开后倒入放有莼菜的汤碗中撒上胡椒粉、淋油，将做好的鸳鸯放在上面即成。

特点：形象逼真，造形美观

口味：汤鲜、味香、脆滑

Mandarin Duck and Water Shield Soup

Ingredients:
150 grams (0.33 lb) water shield (a plant grown on water in warm regions in south China. Water shields from West Lake are most famous.)
20 grams (2/3 oz) ham
2 egg white
4 grams (1/7 oz) carrot
4 grams (1/12 oz) black sesame seeds
3 grams (1/2 tsp) salt
1 gram (1/4 tsp) MSG
1/2 gram (1/10 tsp) pepper powder
5 grams (1 tsp) cooking oil
500 grams (2 cups) chicken soup

Directions:
1. Cut the ham into thin slices. Whip the egg white in a bowl in one direction until thick white foam appears.

2. Put some egg white in a teaspoon, use a dinner knife to shape the egg white into shape of a mandarin duck. Cut a small thin slice off the carrot to serve as a wing of the mandarin duck. Use a sesame seed to represent the eye. Repeat this process to produce a number of mandarin duck shapes. Put them in a steamer and steam for 1 to 2 seconds once the water in the steamer starts to boil.

3. Put 1, 500 g (3 cups) of water in a pot and when this boils, put in the water shield to quick-boil so that the leaves turn bright green. Take out and drain off the water, then put the water shield in a soup bowl.

4. Put chicken soup in the pot, add the ham, salt and MSG, and bring to a boil. Pour into the soup bowl with the quick-boiled water shield in it. Sprinkle on the pepper powder and cooking oil. Place the pre-made mandarin ducks in the soup.

Features: The mandarin ducks made from egg white are vivid and beautiful to look at.
Taste: The soup is delicious and the water shields are succulent.

鸳鸯莼菜汤
Mandarin Duck and Water Shield Soup

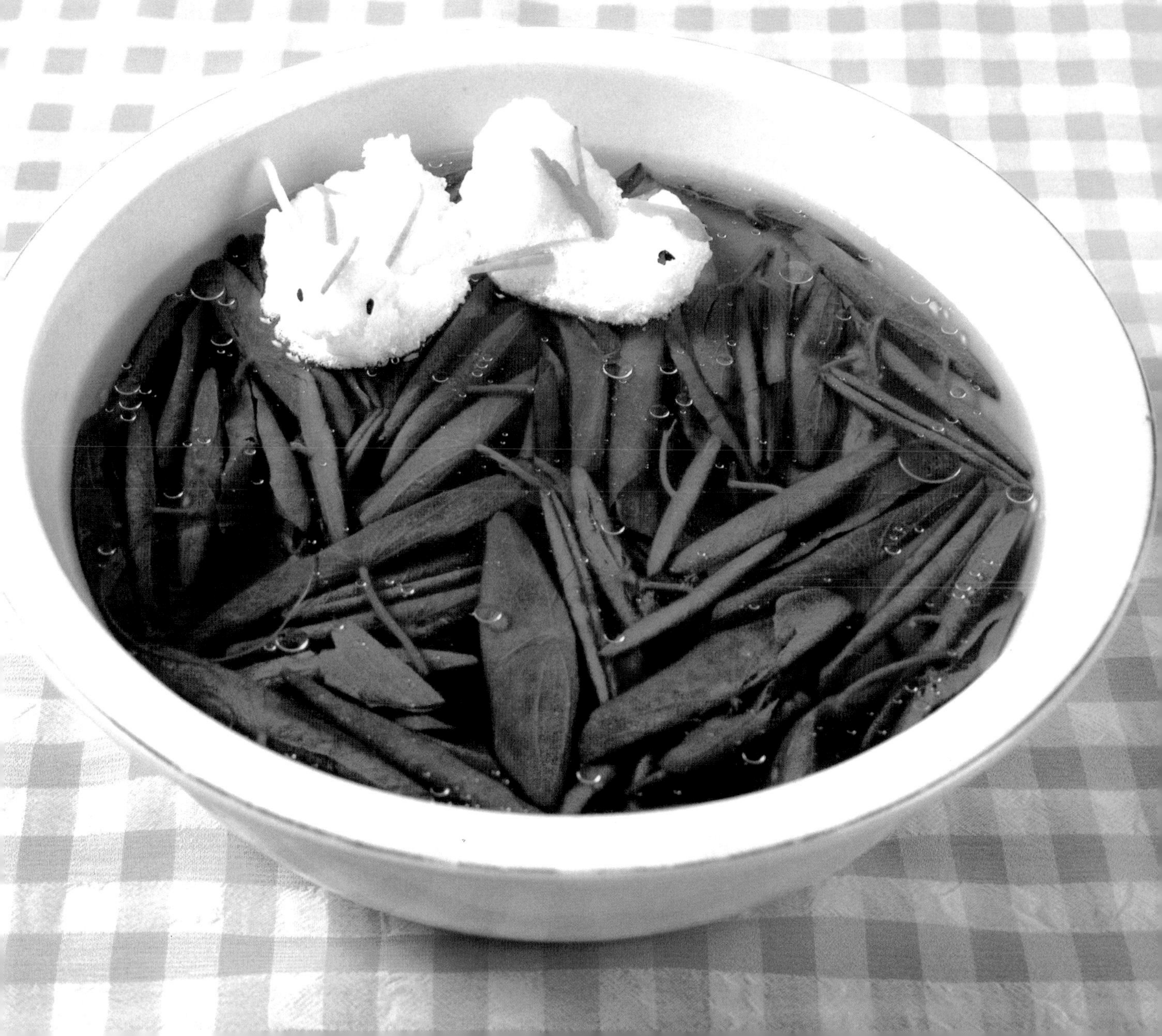

5－7人宴席（B）

第一道菜：荤素五拼盘
第二道菜：宫灯虾仁
第三道菜：火腿湘莲
第四道菜：龙井鱼片
第五道菜：太极双丝
第六道菜：蛋皮烧麦
第七道菜：蘑菇菜心
点　　心：三鲜蒸饺
主　　食：寿桃包子
　汤：　三丝清汤

荤素五拼盘

凉拌葱油海蛰，蒜茸拌黄瓜，白斩鸡，咸菜毛豆，油爆大虾

Family Feast for 5 to 7 People

(Type B)

Course 1: Assorted Five Appetizers
Course 2: Shrimp in Lantern Shape
Course 3: Ham with Lotus Seed
Course 4: Dragon Well Fish Slices
Course 5: Pork with Vegetables
Course 6: Steamed Dumpling Wrapped with Egg
Course 7: Green Vegetables with Mushrooms
Pastry: Steamed Dumpling with Pork and Shrimp
Staple Food: Steamed Longevity Peach
Soup: Combination Meat Shreds Soup

Assorted Five Appetizers

Shredded Jelly Fish with Scallion Oil, Cucumber with Mashed Garlic, Soy Tender Chicken, Salted Tender Soy Beans and Stir-fried Prawns

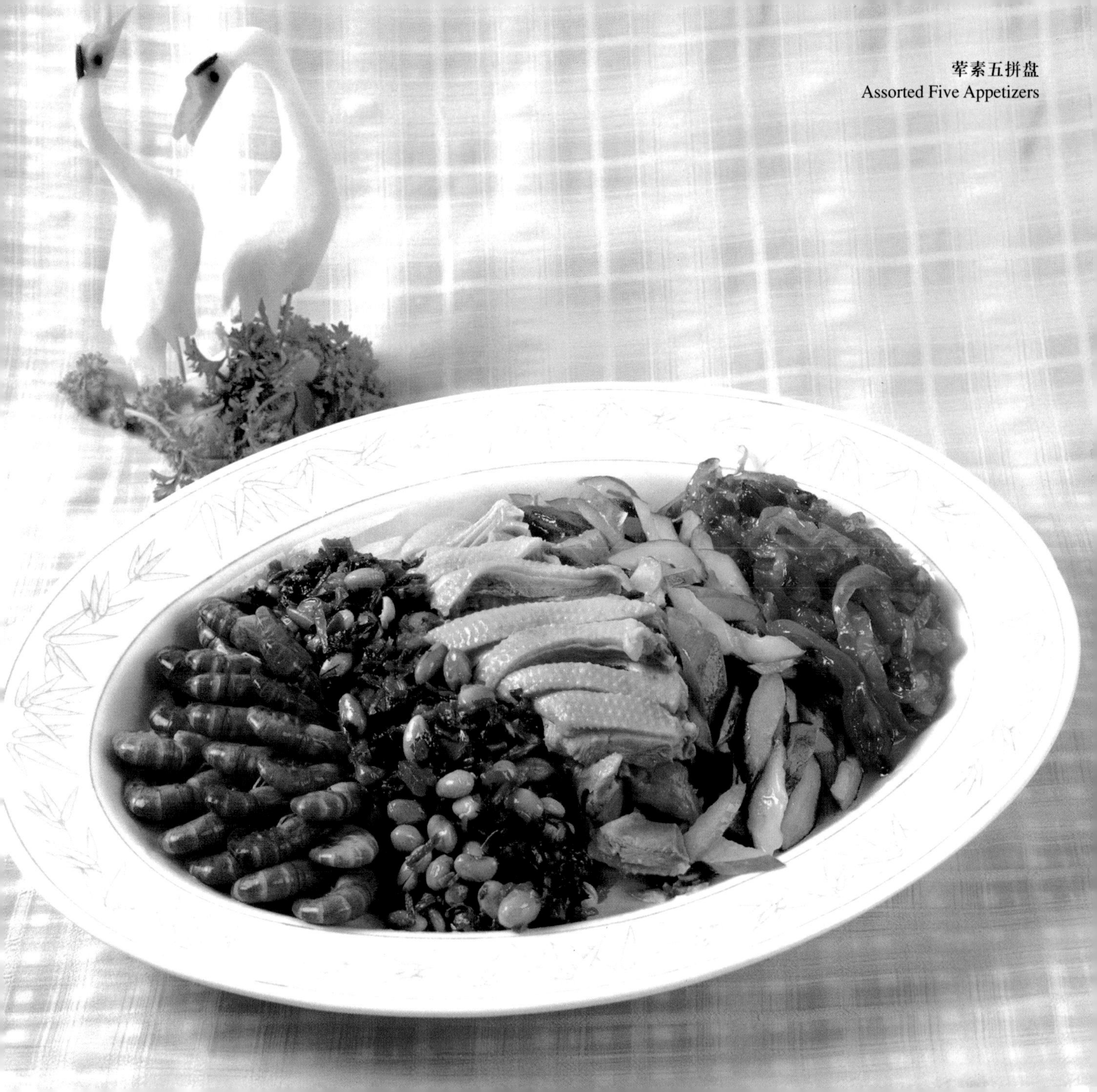

荤素五拼盘
Assorted Five Appetizers

宫灯虾仁

主料：虾仁 450 克

辅料：黄瓜 50 克、胡萝卜 30 克、鸡蛋 3 只

调料：盐 3 克、味精 1 克、料酒 5 克、油 500 克（实耗 50 克）、淀粉 10 克

制作：①虾仁洗净、滤干水份、放鸡蛋清 1 只、盐 3 克、淀粉上浆备用。

②2 只鸡蛋打散、锅放在火上烧热后用一块布浸一些油在锅里擦一下，使锅内均匀沾上一层油，再改开小火，倒入鸡蛋，转动锅子使蛋液在锅里流动成一个圆，成蛋皮，待四周烘干翘起后用手揭下。然后卷起切成细状，做灯笼的飘带。

③黄瓜、胡萝卜切片，在盘中摆出灯笼的形状。

④锅放在火上烧热加油，待油温升至五成热时倒入浆好的虾仁，滑炒至熟后倒出滤油。

⑤锅内留余油 5 克，加料酒、味精，倒入虾仁翻炒后出锅装入盘内的宫灯中即可。

特点：形似宫灯

口味：咸鲜滑嫩

Shrimp in Lantern Shape

Ingredients：
450 grams (1 lb) shelled shrimps
50 grams (0.11 lb) cucumbers
30 grams (1 oz) carrot
3 eggs
3 grams (1/2 tsp) salt
1 gram (1/4 tsp) MSG
5 grams (1 tsp) cooking wine
500 grams (2 cups) oil (only 50 g or 3 1/2 tbsp to be consumed)
10 grams (1 1/2 tbsp) dry cornstarch

Directions：
1. Wash the shrimps clean and drain off the water. Marinate with 1 egg white, 3 g (1/2 tsp) of salt and cornstarch.

2. Whip the two remaining eggs. Put a few drops of oil in a wok and spread it around evenly. Turn the fire low and put in the whipped eggs. Turn the wok slowly so that the eggs form a round wrapping. Take egg wrapping out and roll it up. Cut into thin shreds to resemble the tassels of the lantern.

3. Cut the cucumber and carrot into thin slices and place them on a plate in the form of a palace lantern.

4. Heat the oil to 110-135℃ (230-275℉) and put in the shrimps to stir-fry until they are done. Take out and drain off the oil.

5. Keep 5 g (1 tsp) of oil in the wok. Add the cooking wine and MSG, and put in the stir-fried shrimps. Stir several times and then place in the middle of the lantern shape on the plate.

Features：The dish resembles a beautiful palace lantern.
Taste：Salty, slippery and delicious.

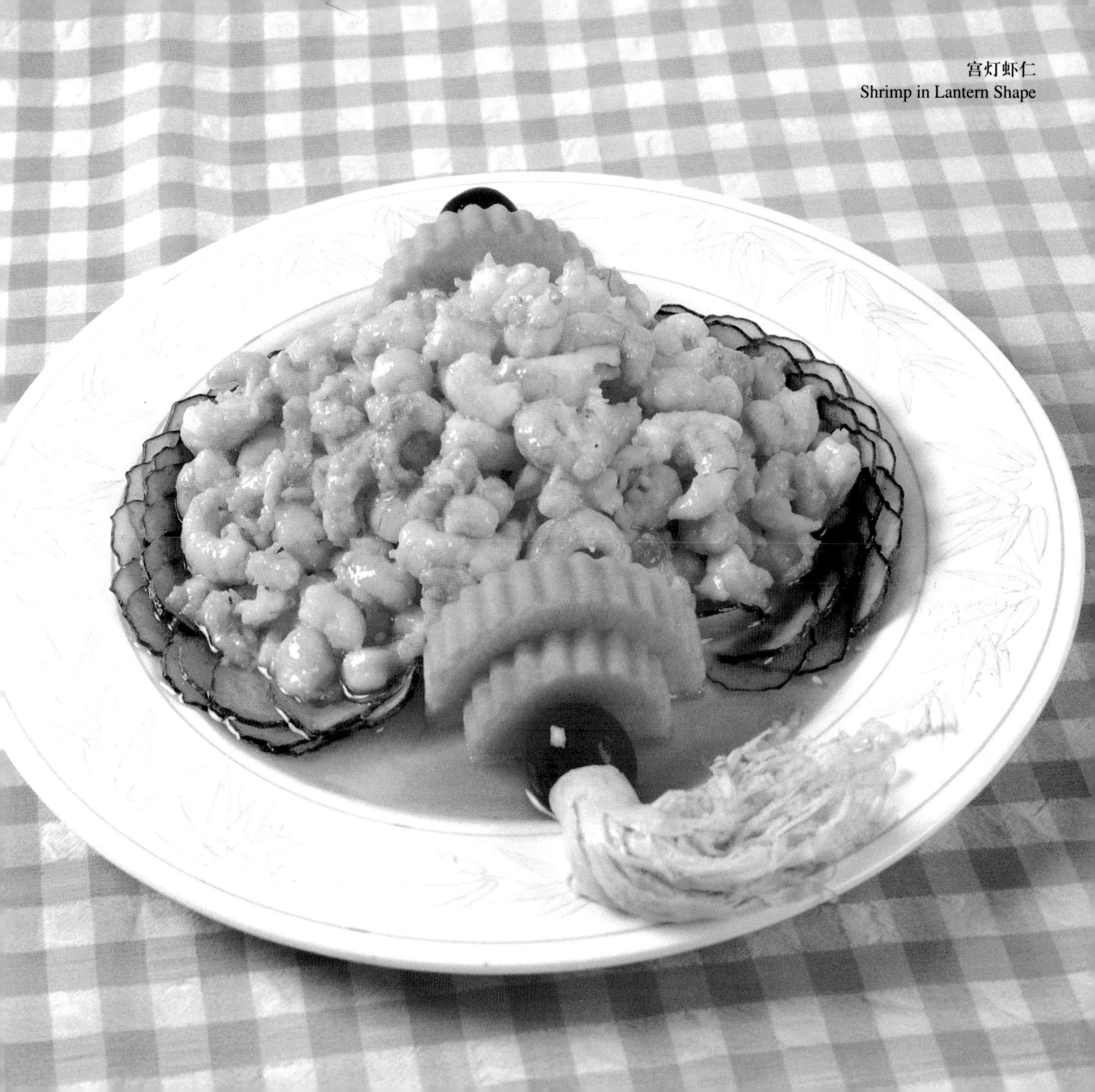

宫灯虾仁
Shrimp in Lantern Shape

火腿湘莲

主料：火腿约 150 克、莲心 250 克

辅料：

调料：糖 50 克、味精 1 克、鸡汤 150 克、湿淀粉 10 克、油 10 克、香菇 1 只

制作：①将莲心放在碗中加满清水上笼蒸熟，香菇放在水中浸泡后剪去老根，火腿用开水洗净后上笼蒸熟。

②取碗一只，在碗里均匀地抹上一层猪油。碗底放上香菇、火腿切成长 10 厘米、宽 2 厘米、厚约 0.2 厘米的薄片，然后将火腿排码在香菇四周。

③把蒸好的莲心放在火腿上，放糖、味精、鸡汤、再上笼蒸 10 分钟左右取下，用平铲按住莲心，倒出汤汁后，把碗扣在盘中，这样莲心就被火腿包住了。

④锅放在火上倒入汤汁，放入温淀粉勾欠后浇在火腿上就成了。

特点：刀功精细、形似馒头

口味：咸中带甜、香味扑鼻

Ham with Lotus Seed

Ingredients：
150 grams (0.33 lb) ham
250 grams (0.55 lb) lotus seeds
50 grams (3 4/5 tbsp) sugar
1 gram (1/4 tsp) MSG
150 grams (10 tbsp) chicken soup
10 grams (2 tsp) mixture of cornstarch and water
10 grams (2 tsp) cooking oil
1 mushroom

Directions：
1. Put the lotus seeds in a bowl and fill it up with water. Steam them until they are done. Soak the mushroom and remove the stem. Wash the ham with hot water and steam it until it is done.

2. Rub a bowl with a layer of lard or oil. Put the mushroom in the bottom of the bowl. Cut the ham into slices 10 cm (4 inches) long, 2 cm (0.8 inch) wide and 0.2 cm (0.08 inch) thick. Neatly place the ham slices around the mushroom.

3. Put the steamed lotus seeds on the ham slices. Add sugar, MSG and chicken soup, and steam for 10 minutes. Hold the lotus seeds in place with a small turning shovel in order to pour out the sauce. Put the contents in the bowl onto a plate by turning the bowl upside down on the plate so as to have the ham covering the lotus seeds.

4. Heat the sauce in a wok. Add the cornstarch-water mixture to thicken it and then sprinkle it on the ham.

Features：With finely cut ham on top, the dish looks like a nice meat bun.
Taste：Salty with a sweet touch and very delicious.

火腿湘莲
Ham with Lotus Seed

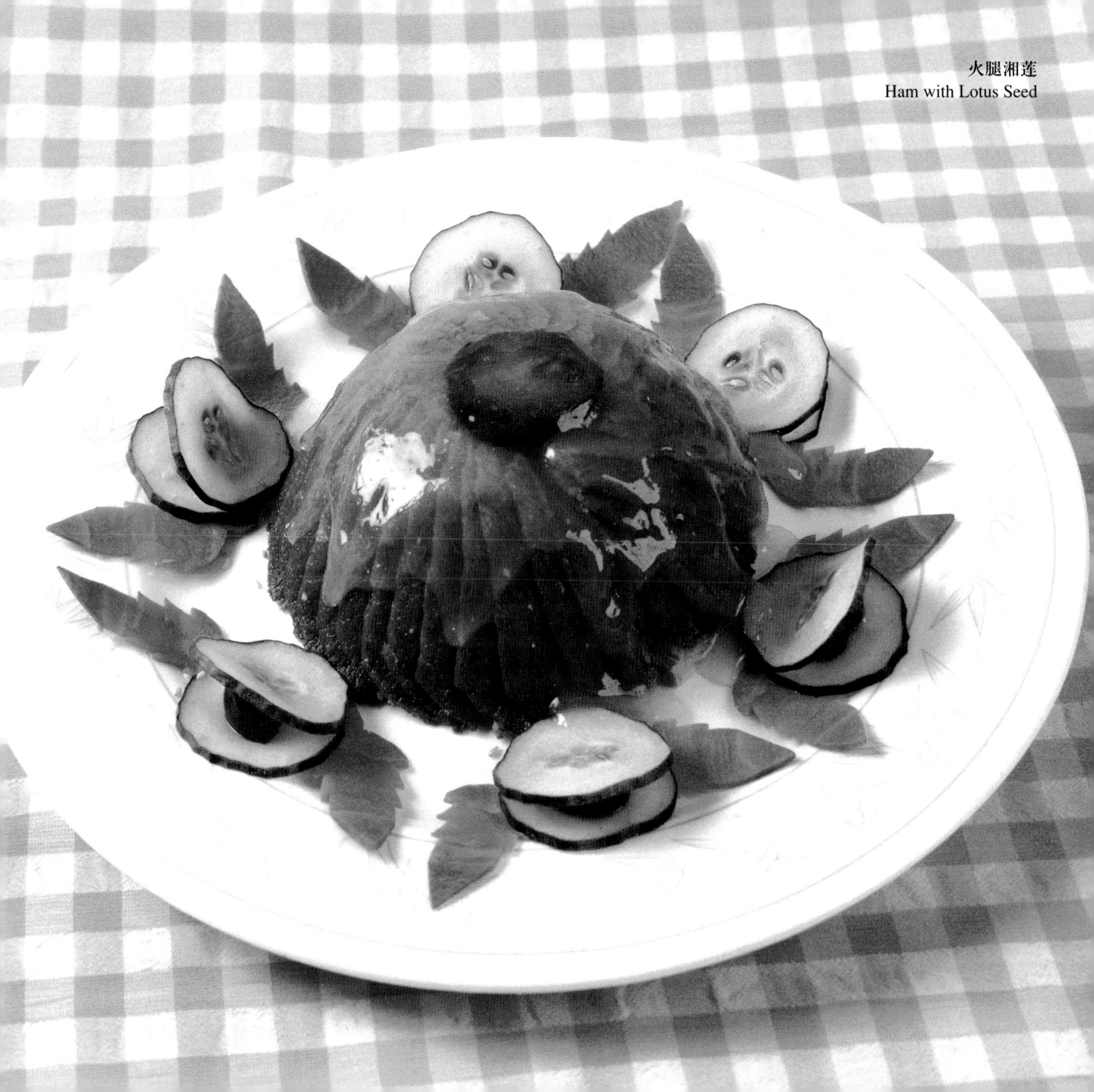

龙井鱼片

主料：草鱼鱼片 300 克。

辅料：龙井茶叶（其它绿菜也可）1 克。

调料：鸡蛋清 1 只、清汤 50 克、料酒 10 克、盐 5 克、味精 1 克、湿淀粉 20 克，油 250 克，淀粉 10 克。

制作：①取去头、尾，除去骨、刺和皮的鱼肉，切成厚约 0.3 毫米，长 5 厘米，宽 4 厘米左右的片。
②用鸡蛋清、盐 2 克，淀粉同鱼片一起上浆备用。茶叶用 50 克沸水泡开后去水，留茶叶待用。
③旺火热锅，锅内加油，待油温升至 5 成熟时，改中火，投入鱼片滑炒至熟，倒出。锅内加余油 10 克烧热，倒入清汤、味精、盐 3 克，调好味，勾芡，倒入鱼片、茶叶翻炒，淋油出锅装盘即可。

特点：茶叶清香，色泽悦目

口味：肉质鲜嫩

Dragon Well Fish Slices

Ingredients：
300 grams (0.66lb) freshwater fish (preferably grass carp) slices
1 gram (1tsp) Dragon Well Tea (or other kind of green tea)
1 egg white
50 grams (3tbsp) water
10 grams (2tsp) cooking wine
5 grams (5/6tsp) salt
1 gram (1/4tsp) MSG
20 grams (1tbsp) cornstarch-water mixture
250 grams (1 cup) cooking oil
10 grams (1 1/2tbsp) dry cornstarch

Directions：
1. Cut the headless, tailless, boneless and skinless fish into slices of about 3 mm (0.12 inch) thick, 5 cm (2 inches) long and 4 cm (1.5 inches) wide.

2. Apply the mixture of the egg white, 2 g (1/3tsp) of salt and cornstarch onto the fish slices. Put 50 g (3tbsp) of hot water into a pot to boil the tea, pour out the water and keep the tea leaves for later use.

3. Use a hot fire to heat the oil in the wok to about 110-135℃ (230-275℉). Now change to a medium fire, throw in the fish slices and stir-fry them. Then move them onto a plate. Heat 10 g (2tsp) of oil in the wok, add in the water, MSG, and 3 g (1/2tsp) of salt. Add the mixture of cornstarch and water to thicken the sauce. Put in the fish slices and tea leaves to stir-fry. Spread some sesame oil in the wok and put the dish on a plate to serve.

Features： The tea leaves give a refreshing and fragrant taste and add color to the delightful dish.

Taste： The meat is very tender.

龙井鱼片
Dragon Well Fish Slices

太极双丝

主料：猪瘦肉 250 克、土豆 150 克

辅料：青椒 2 只

调料：盐 3 克、味精 1 克、豆瓣酱 20 克，料酒 5 克、葱姜末各 2 克、油 500 克（实耗 50 克）淀粉 10 克、湿淀粉 10 克，鸡汤 100 克、鸡蛋清 1 只

制作：①将猪肉洗净，切成丝放盐 2 克，料酒 5 克，鸡蛋清、淀粉上浆备用。土豆去皮切成丝，青椒去根蒂、籽洗净后切成丝。

②锅放在火上，烧热后倒入油，待油温升至五成热时，放入肉丝滑炒至熟后倒出滤油。锅留余油 10 克，放姜葱末豆瓣酱、味精 0.5 克、鸡汤 50 克、湿淀粉 10 克，调好口味，倒入肉丝翻炒出锅装盘。

③锅洗净后放在火上，放油 20 克，烧至五成热放青椒丝、土豆丝煸炒后放盐 1 克、味精 0.5 克、鸡汤 50 克，烧熟后出锅和肉丝一并排成如照片所示的太极图形状即可。

特点：色彩分明

口味：肉丝香醇，土豆丝清新爽口

Pork with Vegetables

Ingredients:

250 grams (0.55 lb) lean pork

150 gram (0.33 lb) potatoes

2 green peppers

3 grams (1/2 tsp) salt

1 gram (1/4 tsp) MSG

20 grams (1 tbsp) bean paste

5 grams (1 tsp) cooking wine

2 grams (1/15 oz) finely cut scallions

2 grams (1/15 oz) chopped ginger

500 grams (2 cups) oil (only 50 g or 3 1/2 tbsp to be consumed)

10 grams (1 1/2 tbsp) dry cornstarch

10 grams (2 tsp) mixture of cornstarch and water

100 grams (6 tbsp) chicken soup

1 egg white

Directions:

1. Wash the pork clean. Cut it into thin shreds. Add 2 g (1/3 tsp) of salt, 5 g (1 tsp) of cooking wine, the egg white and dry cornstarch to marinate. Remove the skin of the potatoes. Cut the potatoes into thin shreds. Remove the stem and seeds of the green peppers and cut them into thin shreds.

2. Heat the oil to 110-135℃ (230-275°F). Add the pork shreds to stir-fry until they are done. Take out and drain off the oil. Keep 10 g (2 tsp) of oil in the wok. Add the scallions, ginger, bean paste, 1/2 g (1/8 tsp) of MSG, 50 g (3 tbsp) of chicken soup and 10 g (2 tsp) of cornstarch-water mixture, and stir. Add the pork shreds and mix. Take out and put on a plate.

3. Wash the wok. Put in 20 g (1 1/2 tbsp) of oil and heat to 110-135℃ (230-275°F). Stir-fry the shredded green peppers and potatoes. Add the remaining salt, MSG and chicken soup and stir until it is done. Put the shredded vegetables on the same plate and arrange the vegetables and pork shreds in a pattern like a Chinese diagram of the "supreme ultimate"(yin and yang). (See picture)

Features: Beautifully shaped.

Taste: The pork shreds are rich, while the potato shreds are refreshing.

太极双丝
Pork with Vegetables

蛋皮烧卖

主料：鸡蛋 5 只，不带皮的硬肋猪肉（去肋骨）200 克

调料：盐 3 克、味精 1 克、料酒 10 克、油 10 克、葱姜末各 3 克、淀粉 10 克、鸡汤 100 克

制作：①将鸡蛋放入碗内打散。锅放在火上，烧热后用一块洁布浸油在锅里擦一下，使锅内均匀地沾上一层油，后改开小火倒 1 匙鸡液，转动锅子，使鸡液在锅里流动成一个直径约为 10 厘米左右的圆型蛋皮，待四周烘干翘起后，用手揭下。用同样方法把鸡液做完备用。

②将猪肉洗净，剁成肉茸，放盐 2 克、味精 0.5 克、料酒、葱姜末拌匀成肉馅。

③将做好的蛋皮正面拍上淀粉，包入肉馅，中部用手指微微捏紧，使上部收口处成开花状。放在盘中上笼蒸熟取下。

④锅放在火上，倒入鸡汤放盐 1 克、味精 0.5 克、用湿淀粉勾欠，然后浇在烧麦开口处并点缀即可。

特点：形似点心，实为菜肴

口味：咸淡适宜

Steamed Dumpling Wrapped with Egg

Ingredients：

5 eggs
200 grams (0.44 lb) boneless streaky pork
3 grams (1/2 tsp) salt
1 gram (1/4 tsp) MSG
10 grams (2 tsp) cooking wine
10 grams (2 tsp) cooking oil
3 grams (1/10 oz) finely cut scallions
3 grams (1/10 oz) chopped ginger
10 grams (1 1/2 tbsp) dry cornstarch
100 grams (7 tbsp) chicken soup

Directions：

1. Whip the eggs. Heat the wok and apply a thin layer of oil. Turn to a low fire and add one tsp of whipped egg. Rotate the wok to make an egg wrapping about 10 cm (4 inches) in diameter. When the edge of the egg wrapping is dry, take it out. Repeat the process until all the whipped eggs are used.

2. Wash the pork clean, grind it, add 2/3 of the salt, half of the MSG, and all the cooking wine, ginger and scallions to mix into a meat filling.

3. Dust the egg wrappings with cornstarch. Put on some meat filling and fold the wrappings into flower shaped dumplings. Steam them until they are done.

4. Put the wok over a fire, Add the chicken soup and remaining salt and MSG. Thicken it with the mixture of cornstarch and water and sprinkle this on the top openings of the dumplings.

Features：Though the dumplings look more like staple food, they are really a side dish.

Taste：Salty to the right taste.

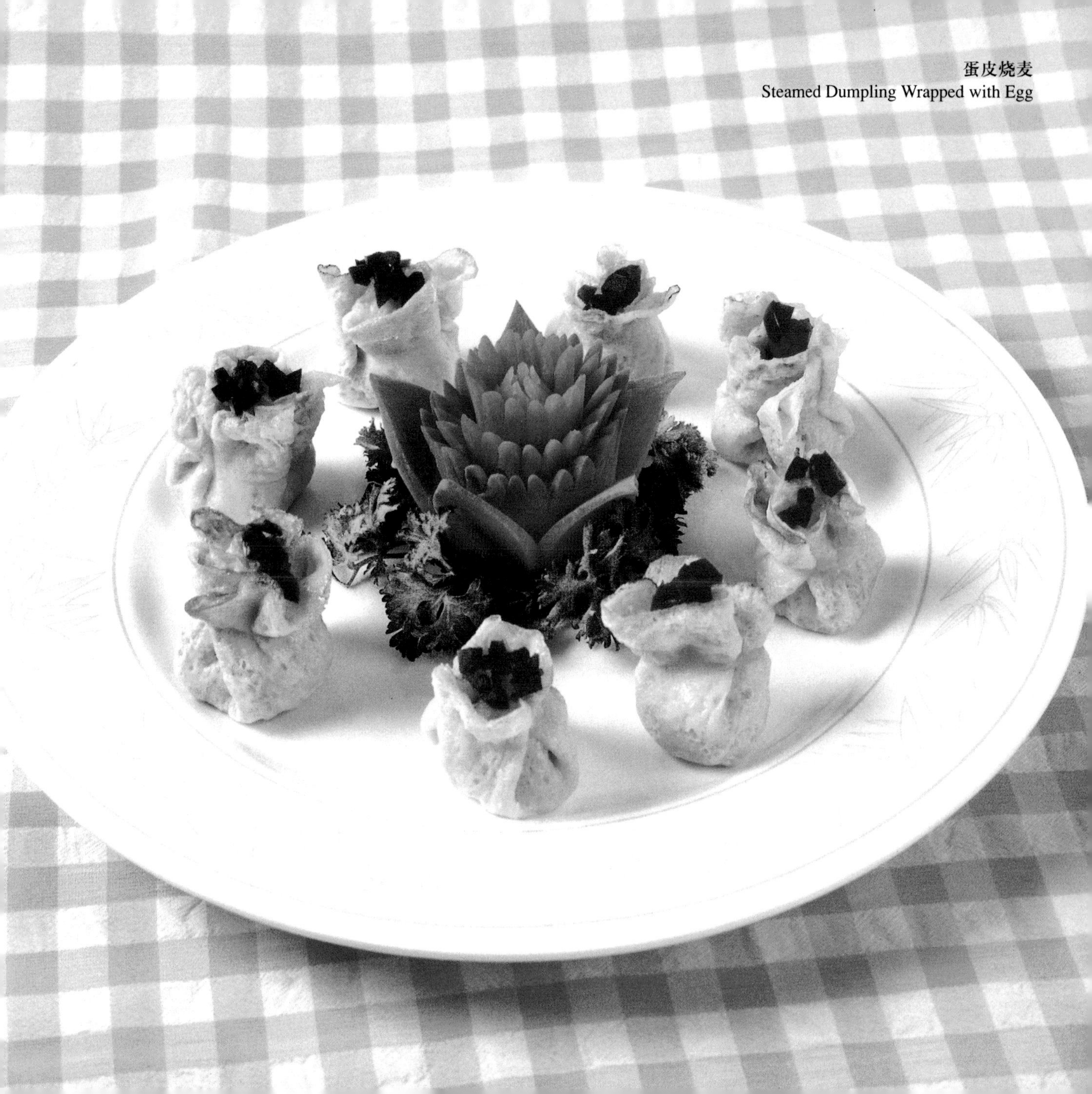

蛋皮烧麦
Steamed Dumpling Wrapped with Egg

蘑菇菜心

主料：青菜心 300 克

辅料：鲜蘑菇 150 克

调料：油 40 克、盐 2 克、味精 1 克、湿淀粉 5 克

制作：①将菜心和蘑菇洗净。

②炒锅置旺火上烧热，放入 30 克油，待油热后倒入菜心煸炒 1 分钟，放入清汤 30 克、盐 1 克、味精 0.6 克，烧 5 分钟至熟出锅装盘。

③原锅置火上，放入 10 克油烧热，倒入蘑菇煸炒 1 分钟，放入清汤 20 克、盐 1 克、味精 0.4 克，烧 3 分钟用湿淀粉勾芡，出锅倒在菜心上即成。

特点：色泽碧绿

口味：鲜嫩清淡

Green Vegetables with Mushrooms

Ingredients：

300 grams (0.66 lb) green vegetables (Chinese rape)
150 grams (0.33 lb) fresh mushrooms
40 grams (3 tbsp) cooking oil
2 grams (1/3 tsp) salt
1 gram (1/4 tsp) MSG
5 grams (1 tsp) mixture of cornstarch and water

Directions：

1. Wash the vegetables and mushrooms clean.

2. Keep the wok over a strong fire. Add 30 g (2 tbsp) of cooking oil. Heat the oil and stir-fry the vegetables for 1 minute. Add 30 g (2 tbsp) of water, 1 g (1/6 tsp) of salt, and half of the MSG. Stir-fry for 5 minutes. Put the vegetables on a plate.

3. Put the remaining 10 g of cooking oil in the wok. Heat it and put in the mushrooms. Stir-fry for 1 minute. Add 20 g (1 1/2 tbsp) of water, 1 g (1/6 tsp) of salt, the remaining MSG, and cook for 3 minutes. Stir the mixture of cornstarch and water well and sprinkle mixture on the mushrooms. Then put the mushrooms on the vegetables and serve.

Features：Tender and green.
Taste：Refreshing.

三鲜蒸饺

主料：面粉 500 克

辅料：猪肉末 250 克、虾仁 100 克

调料：酱油 20 克、糖 5 克、盐 5 克、味精 2 克、麻油 5 克、葱花 10 克、姜末 3 克、料酒 10 克

制法：①虾仁加 2 克盐、1 克味精、5 克麻油、5 克葱花拌匀待用。

②肉末加入剩余的调料拌匀后，再加 50 克水，用力顺一个方向搅拌直至有韧劲，即成馅心。

③面粉加沸水 150 克，拌匀揉透，稍凉后，搓成圆条，摘成每只 15 克的坯子，揿扁，擀成圆形皮子，放上馅心，对折，将中间和两端捏紧，使其间形成两个孔，并于孔内塞入虾仁，即成蒸饺生坯。

④锅中放水 2500 克烧沸后，上笼蒸 15 分钟即可。

特点：外形美观，味清鲜

口味：咸鲜

Steamed Dumpling with Pork and Shrimp

Ingredients:

500 grams (1.1 lb) wheat flour

250 grams (0.55 lb) minced pork

100 grams (0.22 lb) shelled shrimp (either sea or freshwater)

20 grams (1 tbsp) soy sauce

5 grams (1 tsp) sugar

5 grams (5/6 tsp) salt

2 grams (1/2 tsp) MSG

5 grams (1 tsp) sesame oil

10 grams (1/3 oz) finely cut scallions

3 grams (1/10 oz) chopped ginger

10 grams (2 tsp) cooking wine

Directions:

1. Mix the shelled shrimps well with 2 g (1/3 tsp) of salt, 1 g (1/4 tsp) of MSG, 5 g (1 tsp) of sesame oil and 5 g (1/6 oz) of finely cut scallions and put aside.

2. Mix the minced pork with remaining ingredients. Add 50 g (3 tbsp) of cold water and quickly stir in one direction till the substance becomes sticky.

3. Mix the flour with 150 g (10 tbsp) of boiling water. Wait until the dough cools down, roll it into a long strip, divide into small pieces each weighing 15 g (1/2 oz). Press the pieces into wrappings, put the filling in, fold and seal but leave two small openings, one at each end. Insert shrimp into the opening.

4. Put 2,500 g (10 cups) of water into a steamer and bring the water to a boil, Steam the dumplings for 15 minutes.

Features: Beautiful to look at and refreshingly delicious in the mouth.

Taste: Salty and tasty.

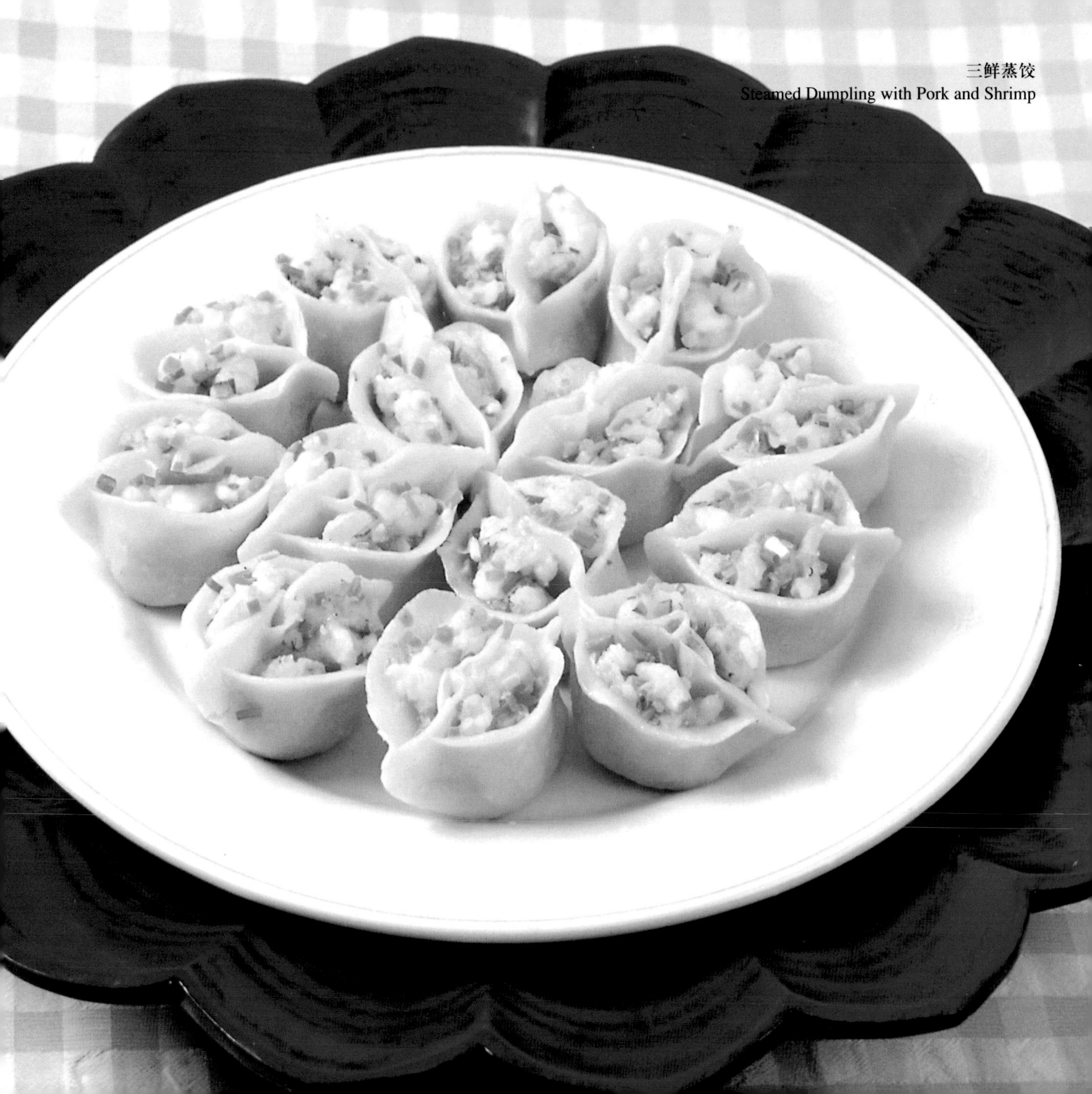

三鲜蒸饺

Steamed Dumpling with Pork and Shrimp

寿桃包子

主料：面粉 250 克、豆沙馅 200 克

辅料：酵母粉、草莓汁 20 克

制法：①面粉加酵母粉拌匀，加入温水拌和成粉团，静置发酵 1 小时。

②将发好的面团揉透，搓成圆长条，按每只 25 克摘坯。

将坯子压扁包入豆沙馅，并收口朝下，再捏成上尖下圆的桃子形状，尖部涂上草莓汁后上笼蒸 10 分钟即可。

特点：松软、美观

口味：香甜

Steamed Longevity Peach

Ingredients：

250 grams (0.55 lb) wheat flour

200 grams (0.44 lb) red bean paste

5 grams (1 tsp) yeast powder

20 grams (1 1/2 tbsp) strawberry juice

Directions：

1. Add the yeast to the flour. Mix the flour with lukewarm water to make a dough. Leave it aside to rise for 1 hour.

2. Shape the dough into a long roll and divide this into pieces each weighing 25 g (5/6 oz). Press each piece flat. Put some red bean paste on top of each piece as filling and then seal and shape pieces into longevity peaches. Rub some strawberry juice on the top to add coloring. Steam for 10 minutes and they are ready to serve.

Features：Soft and beautiful.

Taste：Sweet and delicious.

寿桃包子
Steamed Longevity Peach

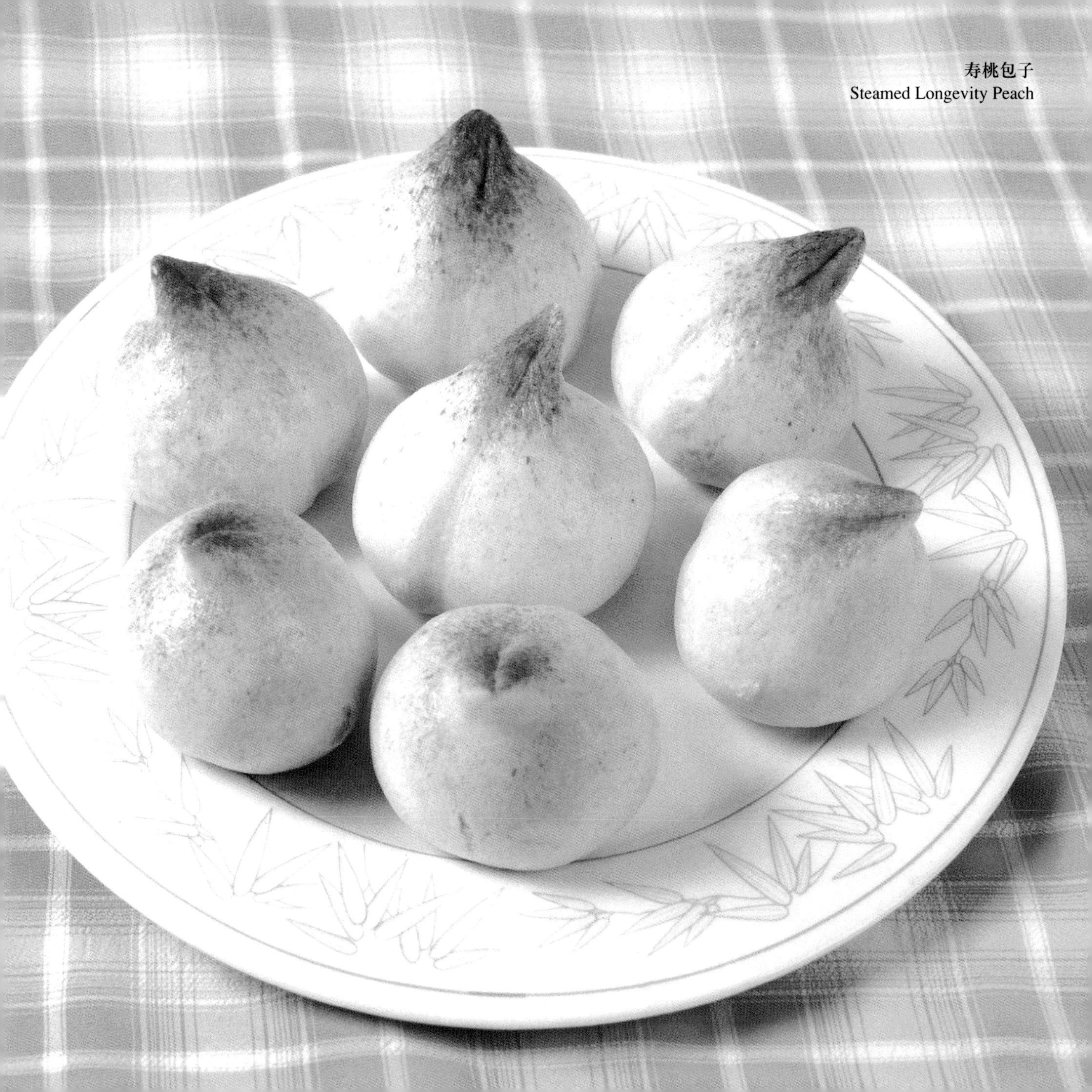

三丝清汤

主料：鸡脯肉 100 克、猪腿肉 100 克

辅料：火腿肉 50 克

调料：料酒 15 克、盐 5 克、味精 2 克、麻油 5 克

制作：①分别将火腿肉、鸡脯肉、猪腿肉切成直径 0.3 厘米，长 6 厘米的细丝。

②锅内放入清水 750 克烧开后，放入三丝、料酒、盐、味精，烧开撇去浮抹，淋油，即成。

特点：汤清肉嫩

口味：鲜美

Combination Meat Shreds Soup

Ingredients：
100 grams (0.22 lb) chicken breast
100 grams (0.22 lb) pork leg
50 grams (0.11 lb) ham
15 grams (3 tsp) cooking wine
5 grams (5/6 tsp) salt
2 grams (1/2 tsp) MSG
5 grams (1 tsp) sesame oil

Directions：
1. Cut the three kinds of meat into shreds of about 1/3 cm (one-tenth of an inch) in diameter and 6 cm (1 1/2 inches) in length.

2. Put 750 g (3 cups) of water in the pot, add the three kinds of meat shreds, cooking wine, salt and MSG. When it reaches boiling point, skim off the foam, sprinkle on the sesame oil and serve.

Features：The soup is clear and the meat tender.
Taste：Very delicious.

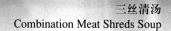

计量换算表

1磅	1盎司	1打兰	1格令
约454克	约28克	约1.8克	约0.06克

ml 勺 \ 调料	水	油	酱油	醋	料酒	盐	味精	砂糖	淀粉
1ml勺	约1克	约0.9克	约1.2克	约1克	约1克	约1.2克	约0.7克	约0.9克	约0.4克
5ml勺	约5克	约4.5克	约6克	约5克	约5克	约6.3克	约3.7克	约4.5克	约2克
15ml勺	约15克	约13.5克	约18克	约15克	约15克	约18.5克	约11克	约13克	约6克
50ml勺	约50克	约55克	约60克	约50克	约50克	约63克		约42克	约20克
500ml勺	约500克	约549克	约600克	约500克	约500克	约630克			

A comparison of the weight systems

US system	1 grain(gr)	1ounce(oz)	1pound(lb)
Metric	0.065 gram(g)	28.35 grams(g)	454 grams(g)

A conversion table for measuring Chinese cooking ingredients*

ingredients \ cornstarch	water	ckg oil	soy sauce	vinegar	ckg wine	salt	MSG	sugar	cornstarch
1 pinch/1ml	1g	0.9g	1.2g	1g	1g	1.2g	0.7g	0.9g	0.4g
1tsp/5ml	5g	4.5g	6g	5g	5g	6.3g	3.7g	4.5g	2g
1tbsp/15ml	15g	13.5g	18g	15g	15g	18.5g	11g	13g	6g
1.76floz/50ml	50g	55g	60g	50g	50g	63g		42g	20g
3.52floz/1cup	500g	549g	600g	500g	500g	630g			

*All figures in grams given here are approximate as the exact equivalents will result in too many digits after the decimal point.

在编辑《学做中国菜》系列丛书的过程中，得到了苏州饭店的大力支持和帮助。作为苏州市旅游业的骨干企业苏州饭店已有数十年的历史，饭店拥有一流的烹饪厨师，经验丰富，技艺精湛。今借此书出版之机，我们对苏州饭店给予的支持，深表感谢!

We wish to thank the Suzhou Hotel, which kindly provided strong support and assistance to the compilation of the *Learn to Cook Chinese Dishes* series. As a major tourist hotel in the city of Suzhou, the Suzhou Hotel has a history of dozens of years and is serviced by experienced first-class chefs.

图书在版编目（CIP）数据

学做中国菜·家宴类/《学做中国菜》编委会编.-北京：外文出版社，2000
ISBN 7-119-02628-3

Ⅰ.学… Ⅱ.学… Ⅲ.家宴-烹饪-中国-汉、英对照 Ⅳ.TS972.182

中国版本图书馆 CIP 数据核字（2000）第 07436 号

Members of the Editorial Board:
  Sun Jiaping   Lu Qinpu
  Sun Shuming   Liu Chun'gen
  Lan Peijin
Dish preparation and text:
  Zhu Deming   Wen Jinshu
  Zhu Guifu   Zhang Guomin
  Zhang Guoxiang   Xu Rongming
  Cao Gang
Editor: Lan Peijin
English translation and editing:
  Huang Youyi   Foster Stockwell   Cong Guoling
Design: Lan Peijin
Photography: Sun Shuming   Liu Chun'gen   Lan Peijin
Cover design: Wang Zhi

编委：孙建平　鲁钦甫　孙树明
　　　　刘春根　兰佩瑾
菜肴制作及撰文：朱德明　温金树
　　　　　　　　朱桂福　张国民
　　　　　　　　张国祥　徐荣明
　　　　　　　　曹　刚
责任编辑：兰佩瑾
英文翻译：黄友义　卓柯达　丛国玲
设计：兰佩瑾
摄影：孙树明　刘春根　兰佩瑾
封面设计：王　志

First Edition 2000

Learn to Cook Chinese Dishes
—Family Banquet

ISBN 7-119-02628-3

©Foreign Languages Press
Published by Foreign Languages Press
24 Baiwanzhuang Road, Beijing 100037, China
Home Page: http://www.flp.com.cn
E-mail Addresses：info @ flp.com.cn
　　　　　　　　sales @ flp.com.cn
Printed in the People's Republic of China

学做中国菜·家宴类
《学做中国菜》编委会　编
ⓒ　外文出版社
外文出版社出版
（中国北京百万庄大街 24 号）邮政编码 100037
外文出版社网页：http://www.flp.com.cn
外文出版社电子邮件地址：info @ flp.com.cn
　　　　　　　　　　　sales @ flp.com.cn
北京骏马行图文中心制版
天时印刷（深圳）有限公司印制
2000 年（24 开）第一版
2000 年第一版第一次印刷
（英汉）
ISBN 7-119-02628-3/J·1534（外）
08000（精）